Contents

Within each theme, the numbered subsections refer to sections of the CCEA Specification.

Author's note

This revised edition would not have been possible without the help and support of the following people: Bill Polley, Aileen Corbett (Glastry College), Gillian Lawther (Nendrum College, Comber) and Ken Sittlington (Movilla High School,) who reviewed and improved on each chapter; Richard Watson and Lisa McManus at Marble Arch Caves who helped with information for Theme B; Arthur Byrne (St Louis Grammar) who helped in Theme F, and thanks are also due to two former students of his – Catherine Stewart and Deirdre Hamill – whose A level projects enabled me to draw the urban field of Ballymena on page 74; and James McHenry (Dieskirt Farm), Geoffrey Armstrong (Tullyhona Farm), Patsy McBride (Watertop Farm), Stephen Butler and Andy McCrea (Action Renewables), Helen Barnes (Laganside), Vicki Smyth (Titanic Quarter), Gillian Hunt (Woodland Trust), Jake and Charles Grieves-Cook (Porini), Trevor Field (Roundabout), and Margaret McMullan (CCEA), who all took time out of their busy schedules and put up with my endless questions with patience and good humour. Finally I want to thank my wife Tanya, who again was deprived of my company while I worked at this book.

I would like to dedicate this book to three Geography teachers – Trevor Carleton, Paddy Turk and Brian Hurl – who inspired me at Campbell College in the early 1960s. Their enthusiasm and love for the subject started me on the long road to this publication.

Derek Polley, April 2005

Derek Polley, MEd, BA, Dip Ed, DASE, is Head of Geography at Nendrum College, Comber. He graduated with a BA from Queen's University, Belfast, in 1969 and added a Diploma in Education in 1970. He taught for two years in Sierra Leone. He has also taught in Ballynahinch High, Movilla High and Knockbreda High before being appointed to Comber High School (now Nendrum College) in 1991. This has given him wide experience of teaching Geography to the Junior School and also at CSE, 'O' level, GCSE and 'A' level. His first book, Home Ground, for Key Stage 3, was published by Colourpoint in 1999.

He can be e-mailed at derek_polley@hotmail.com

A list of useful web sites mentioned in this book can be found at www.colourpoint.co.uk/extra/widerground

THEME A

Atmosphere and Human Impact

This theme concentrates on selected aspects of meteorology which illustrate a range of processes and the interrelationships between people and natural environment including management issues. Both hazardous and favourable effects of atmospheric processes should be considered.

This is not a common sight in Northern Ireland; usually there is too much water.

The key to understanding weather is to understand what happens in the atmosphere. This is the layer of air which surrounds the Earth. It is composed of a mixture of gases including oxygen (21%), nitrogen (78%), and other gases. These other gases include water vapour.

All our weather is powered by the sun which heats the atmosphere. Day-to-day changes in the atmosphere are called weather. These are measured and recorded by weather instruments. The results are fed to the Met Office computers in Bracknell, England and plotted on a synoptic chart (weather map) – see pages 8, 10 and 24. Once the map has been drawn, the meteorologist tries to forecast what will happen in the future.

The weather records are stored and help to build up a picture of what the pattern is over the year. Readings are taken for at least thirty years and averaged out to give the climate.

Weather and climate are different. Weather is the day-to-day changes in the atmosphere around us while climate is the pattern over the year.

1.1 Elements of the weather, units of measurement and instruments

Weather

Weather is something that affects everybody. Some people have jobs that are easier or harder depending on the weather. Pupils going to and from school are affected by the weather. Sports, games and transport are affected by the weather. Walking the dog, doing a paper round, drying washing or shopping are all easier if the weather is dry and warm. Cold and wet weather makes all these things harder. In some cases extreme weather can result in loss of life and millions of pounds of damage which has to be put right. Strong winds damage trees and houses, heavy rain causes floods, and freezing temperatures cause accidents and put up fuel bills for everybody.

Recording the weather

Weather is made up of different things such as rain, wind and temperature. These are called the elements of weather, and they all have to be measured and recorded. There are five elements that most people will know about, but a **meteorologist** will look at other elements as well. Resource A shows the instruments used to measure these elements.

Resource A

Rainfall/Precipitation: this is measured in mm using a rain gauge. Precipitation can be shortened to PPT.

Temperature: this is measured in degrees Celsius (°C) using a maximum–minimum thermometer.

Wind speed: this is measured in km per hour using a anemometer.

Cloud cover: this is measured in eighths or oktas using observation.

Wind direction: this is measured with the points of the compass using a wind vane or wind sock.

The box above is called a **Stevenson Screen**.
It holds the thermometers and keeps them out of the direct rays of the sun.

A meteorologist will want to know other things as well. When he puts all this information together then he will be able to predict the weather and issue a forecast for the daily newspapers, television and the internet. Resource B shows some of the other elements and instruments.

Resource B ▼

The type of cloud is useful; this is measured by observation. There are ten different types of cloud, but they are based on three basic ones: cirrus, stratus and cumulus.

Sunshine is measured in hours using a sunshine recorder.

Visibility is measured in metres or kilometres using observation.

Air pressure, or weight of air, is measured in millibars using a barometer.

1.2 Air masses

The weather over Northern Ireland is influenced by four main air masses. They are shown in Resource C. Each of these air masses gives a particular pattern of weather depending on the time of year. Polar air is cold and comes from the north. Tropical air is warm and comes from the south. Maritime air is moist because it comes from the west over the Atlantic Ocean. Continental air is dry because it comes from the east over the continent of Europe.

Polar Maritime (PM)

This is cold moist air which has travelled down from the Arctic and picked up some moisture on the way. It is our second most common air mass. In summer it brings us sunny intervals and scattered showers, giving temperatures of 10–14°C. In winter the temperatures are much lower (4–8°C) and the showers may be of sleet or snow. Winds from the north-west are frequently strong and can be up to force 7 or higher. This is the air mass which follows behind a depression.

Resource C

Air masses which affect the British Isles

Polar Continental (PC)

This is rare in Northern Ireland as it comes from Russia. It occurs only in winter and brings bitterly cold weather with temperatures going below freezing. There is a risk of snow as it can pick up moisture as it crosses the North Sea. It often brings icy weather to the east coast of Britain but, because we are close to the Atlantic Ocean which is relatively warm in winter, it may not reach Northern Ireland — if it does it usually does not last long.

Tropical Maritime (TM)

This is warm moist air which has picked up moisture on its journey over thousands of kilometres of sea. It is our most common air mass occurring roughly 60% of the year. In winter it brings milder weather (8–12°C); in summer it brings warmer temperatures (14–18°C). Whenever we get this air mass we often get low cloud, rain and drizzle. The weather is often humid as the air is saturated with moisture. This is the air mass in the warm sector of a depression.

Tropical Continental (TC)

This air mass is rare in Northern Ireland as it comes from the Sahara Desert. It occurs only in summer and brings a spell of hot dry weather (20°C+). It often reaches the south-east coast of England but because we are close to the Atlantic Ocean, which is relatively cool in summer, it may not reach Northern Ireland — if it does it usually does not last long.

1.3 Reasons for variability in weather patterns

When the meteorologist looks at the weather maps, there are two weather systems which are common throughout the year. The first of these is a depression or area of low pressure. The second of these is an anticyclone or area of high pressure.

The Mourne Mountains with low stratus cloud – the warm sector of a depression

The Mourne Mountains with cumulus cloud – the depression has just passed through

Depression

This is a wave or ripple which travels east along the polar front, the boundary between warmer tropical air to the south and colder polar air to the north. Depressions originate over the Atlantic Ocean and then travel east towards Europe. They usually pass over or close to the United Kingdom. Depressions will reach Northern Ireland first and will affect Tyrone and Fermanagh before they affect Down and Antrim. They bring a certain sequence of weather:

Rising temperatures
Falling pressure
Lowering cloud
Thicker cloud
Wind direction changing
   from south-east to
   north-west
Wind strength increasing
Increased risk of rain

Resource D ▶

Depression crossing the British Isles
© The Met Office

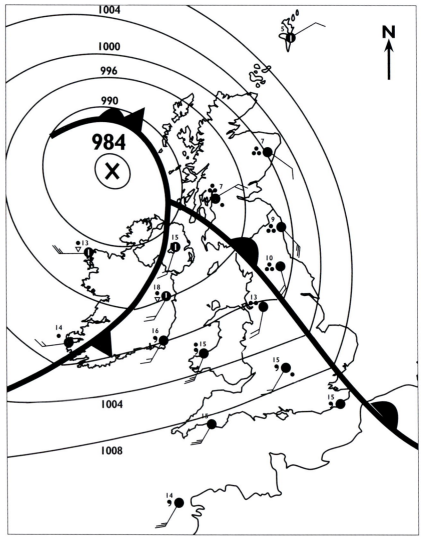

Resource D is a synoptic chart (weather map) for noon on 16 October 1998 and shows a typical depression crossing the British Isles. The centre of the depression is to the north of Ireland and the pressure is 984 millibars. This is giving the British Isles cloud, wind and rain along the warm and cold fronts. Resource E shows a satellite image of this depression.

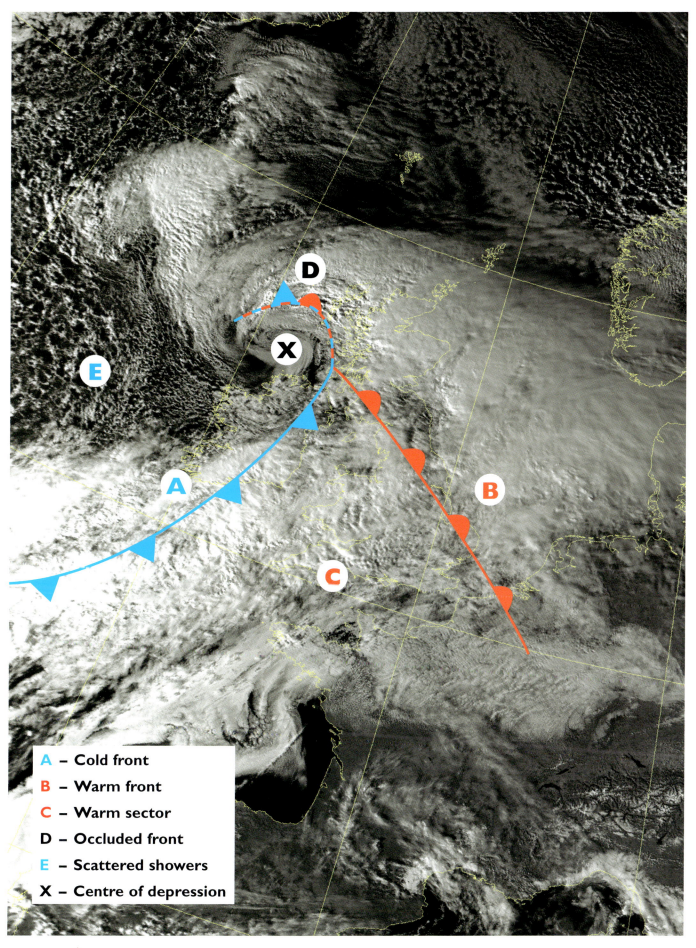

A – Cold front
B – Warm front
C – Warm sector
D – Occluded front
E – Scattered showers
X – Centre of depression

Resource E   A satellite image for 16 October 1998

Anticyclone

This is an area where pressure is high and the air is descending. The air warms as it descends so there is less chance of condensation, cloud and rain. Winds are light and variable in direction. There are no fronts in an anticyclone as there is only one air mass present. Anticyclones develop between depressions and if the pressure is very high they can 'block' depressions and give a long period of fine stable weather.

Winter anticyclones are the same as summer anticyclones when you look at a weather map – the pattern of isobars is the same. The big difference is in the temperature.

Resource F is a synoptic chart for 8 August 1995 at noon. It shows an anticyclone centred over the North Sea with a high pressure of 1028 millibars. This is giving most of the British Isles fine, clear, warm weather with light winds. Resource G shows a satellite image of this anticyclone.

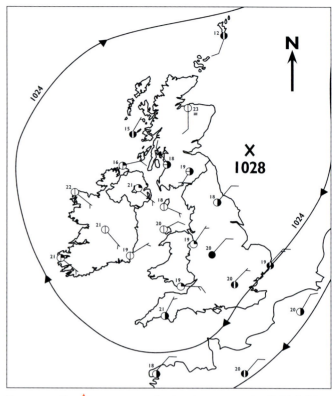

Resource F ▲   Anticyclone over the British Isles
© The Met Office

Mourne Mountains experiencing the fine weather of a summer anticyclone

Mourne Mountains experiencing the cold weather of a winter anticyclone

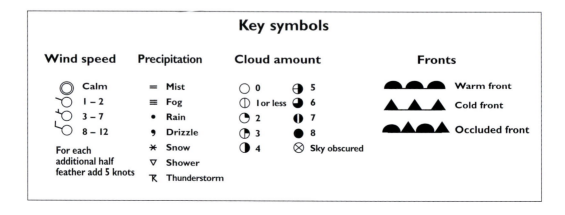

Key symbols

Wind speed	Precipitation	Cloud amount		Fronts
◎ Calm	= Mist	○ 0	◐ 5	●●● Warm front
⊖ 1 – 2	≡ Fog	◑ 1 or less	◕ 6	▲▲▲ Cold front
⊝ 3 – 7	• Rain	◔ 2	◑ 7	▲◠▲ Occluded front
⟋◯ 8 – 12	ˌ Drizzle	◷ 3	● 8	
For each additional half feather add 5 knots	✳ Snow	◐ 4	⊗ Sky obscured	
	▽ Shower			
	ⓚ Thunderstorm			

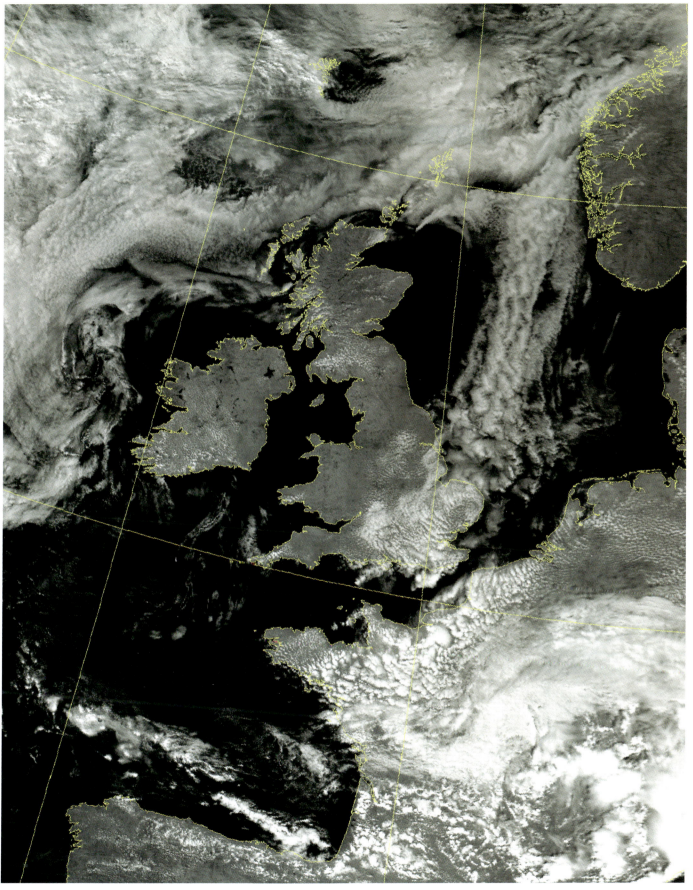

Resource G ▲   A satellite image for 8 August 1995

2.1 Causes of variation in climate: role of latitude, altitude, prevailing winds and continentality on the continent of Europe

These are the four factors which give the variation in climate:

Latitude (distance from the equator)

The closer you are to the equator the hotter it is; the further away you are the colder it is. Resource H shows the Earth divided into simple climate areas. Europe is between 71° and 35° north of the equator so it lies in the temperate zones. That means that the climate of Europe is either warm temperate or cool temperate depending on how far north you go. The very northern part of Europe is right on the edge of the cold zone.

Resource H ▶

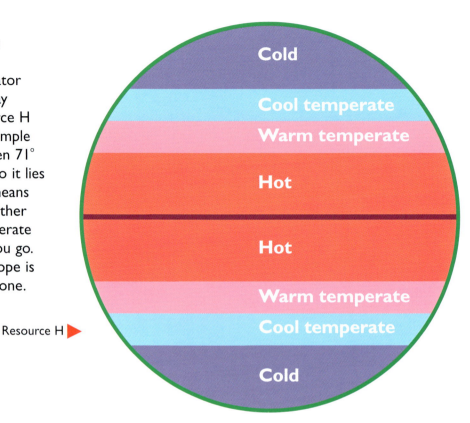

Altitude (height above sea level)

The higher up you go the colder it gets. Every 150 metres you climb the temperature will drop by 1°C. Resource I shows what will happen to the temperature at the top of different mountains in Europe.

Resource I

Mountain	Country	Height in m	Temperature at sea level in °C	Temperature at the top in °C
Slieve Donard	Northern Ireland	850	15	9.5
Ben Nevis	Scotland	1341	15	6
Mont Blanc	France/Italy	4807	20	-12
Rysy	Poland	2499	20	3.5
Kelnekaise	Sweden	2111	10	-4
Mulhacen	Spain	3482	25	2

Prevailing wind (the direction the wind blows most of the time)

In Europe the prevailing wind is from the west or south-west 60% of the time (three days out of five). This wind blows from the Atlantic Ocean, which is a large mass of fairly warm water. The result of this is a wind that is mild in winter and warm in summer. It blows over a large area of sea so it picks up water and gives Europe quite a lot of rain. There are two types of rain which are common in Europe. They both occur as a result of the prevailing wind from the Atlantic Ocean. The first type is relief rain (see Resource J). This happens when moist air from the Atlantic rises, cools and condenses when it blows over Europe.

Resource J ▼

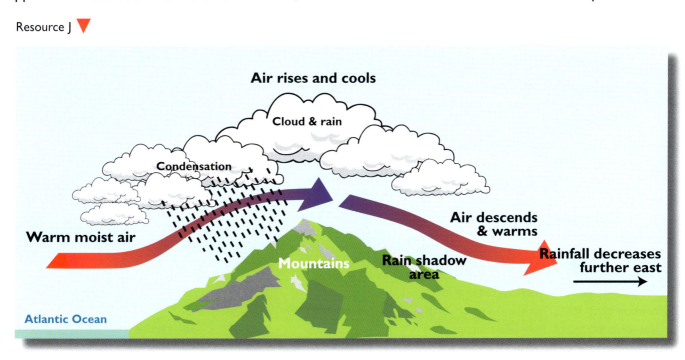

The second type of rain is frontal rain (Resource K). This occurs as depressions push fronts into Europe from the Atlantic. Places on the west coast, closest to the Atlantic Ocean, are affected first and get the heaviest rain. As the front moves east the rain dies out. Frontal rain which reaches mountain areas will also rise, cool and condense to give relief rain. Mountain areas get much more rain than other areas.

Resource K ▼

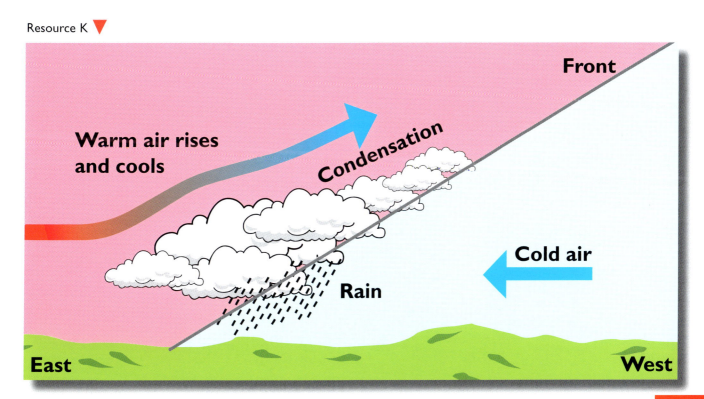

Continentality (the changes in climate away from the influence of the sea)

Look at the table below which shows climate figures for Valentia in Ireland, Berlin in Germany and Warsaw in Poland. Although they are roughly the same latitude and altitude, their climates are very different. Valentia is beside the sea, Berlin is much further inland and Warsaw is still further away from the sea. Resource L shows you where they are located.

Place	January average	July average	Range	Total rainfall
Valentia	7°C	15°C	8°C	1430 mm
Berlin	-1°C	19°C	20°C	581 mm
Warsaw	-4°C	19°C	23°C	550 mm

Resource L

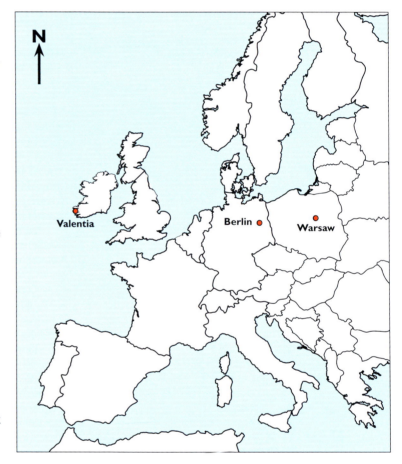

Distance from the Atlantic Ocean is a very important factor in Europe's weather. It has three main effects:

1. As you travel east into Europe the rainfall gets less. The wind which brings Valentia so much rain blows east into Europe and by the time it reaches Berlin and Warsaw it does not have a lot of rain left. You can see that they are much drier.

2. As you travel east into Europe the summer temperatures get warmer.

3. As you travel east into Europe the winter temperatures get colder.

Temperatures change so much because the Atlantic Ocean has a moderating effect on the climate. The sea keeps the coast of Europe (Valentia) cooler in summer and warmer in winter than places further inland (Warsaw).

If we put these four factors together we will have a better understanding of why a particular place has the climate it has. Our case study is the continent of Europe which is the smallest of the seven continents.

It measures 4000 kilometres from the northern tip of Norway to the island of Crete in the south. From Bray Head in the west of Ireland to Sverdlovsk in the Ural Mountains of Russia there is a distance of 5000 kilometres.

The northern part of Norway (latitude 71° north) is inside the Arctic Circle, while the island of Crete (latitude 35° north) is about 300 kilometres north of Africa.

Despite its small size it does not have the same climate all over. It has five climate areas, six if you count the mountain climates of the Alps and the Urals. Resource M overleaf shows a map of Europe with the climate zones marked in and climate graphs of the towns are provided. Even then it is clear that the whole zone does not have the same climate. The southern part of Norway would be quite different from the northern part of Spain, yet on the map they are both marked with a maritime climate.

◀ **Mountain climate.** The climate of the Dolomites in northern Italy is influenced by altitude. Even in mid summer there is snow on the highest peaks. In winter the area is popular with skiers and is a centre for winter sports.

▼ **Mediterranean climate.** The climate of central Italy has hot, dry summers. Temperatures regularly reach 40°C. Plants, animals and people have to adapt to the summer drought.

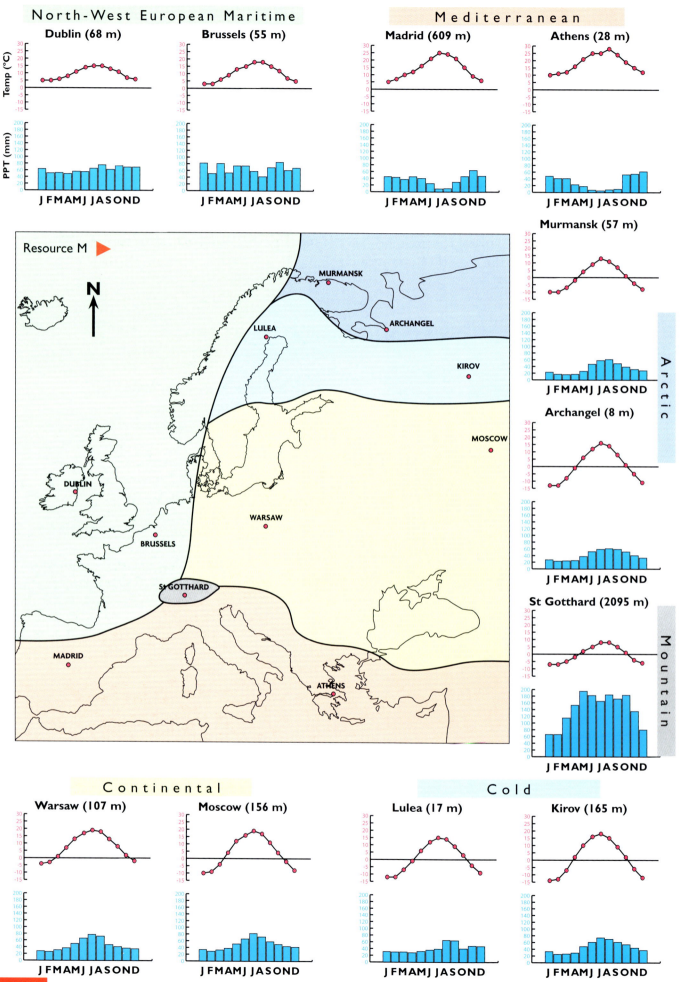

North-West European Maritime

Dublin (68 m)

Brussels (55 m)

Mediterranean

Madrid (609 m)

Athens (28 m)

Murmansk (57 m)

Archangel (8 m)

St Gotthard (2095 m)

Arctic

Mountain

Resource M

N

MURMANSK

ARCHANGEL

LULEA

KIROV

MOSCOW

WARSAW

DUBLIN

BRUSSELS

St GOTTHARD

MADRID

ATHENS

Continental

Warsaw (107 m)

Moscow (156 m)

Cold

Lulea (17 m)

Kirov (165 m)

Summary table of the six climate types

Climate type	Summers	Winters	Precipitation	Comment
NW Maritime	Cool	Mild	Moderate, all year round	Influenced by the prevailing SW/W wind bringing tropical maritime (tm) air from the Atlantic
Mediterranean	Hot & dry	Warm and wet	Light, mainly in winter with a summer drought	Influenced mainly by latitude, but the eastern Mediterranean is warmer and drier than the west
Continental	Hot	Cold	Light with a peak in summer	Influenced by continentality. As you travel east there are hotter summers, colder winters and less rain.
Cold	Cool	Cold	Light with a peak in summer, snow in winter	Influenced by latitude and continentality. These areas are just inside the Arctic Circle so they are cold. As you travel east there are hotter summers, colder winters and less rain.
Arctic	Short and cool	Long and cold	Light with a peak in summer, snow in winter	Influenced by latitude. These areas are well inside the Arctic Circle. Even in summer the sun is low in the sky, while in winter there are long spells of darkness when the sun never shines.
Mountain	Short	Long	Heavy all year round, with snow in winter	The main influence here is altitude. The higher the land, the colder the temperatures and the shorter the growing season.

Each of these climate types presents challenges and difficulties for the farmer.

- The Arctic and Cold climates have a short growing season.
- The Mediterranean climate has a summer drought.
- The Maritime climate has all-year-round rain.
- The Continental climate has extreme temperature ranges.
- Mountain climates have their own problems as the high altitude means lower average temperatures and less rainfall.

2.2 Impact of climate on farming

The Northern Ireland climate can be summed up as cool summers, mild winters, and rain all year. It is part of the North-West Maritime climate (see pages 16 and 17) – that is the area of western Europe which is close to the sea and whose climate is moderated by the Atlantic Ocean. Other descriptions include mild climate (warm and wet) or mild (wet all year, cool summer). Different atlases and textbooks have different descriptions, but in most of these Northern Ireland is usually thought of as having the same climate all over the country.

In fact, people who live there know that there are differences between different parts of Northern Ireland. These differences in climate affect the people who live there – in particular the farmers. This section concentrates on how the weather in two areas dictates the type of farming carried out there. The two farms are located in Glenariff (County Antrim) and Florence Court (County Fermanagh). The following maps show the climate patterns over Northern Ireland (Resources N, O, P, and Q). The positions of the two farms are marked on each map.

Average maximum January temperatures in °C

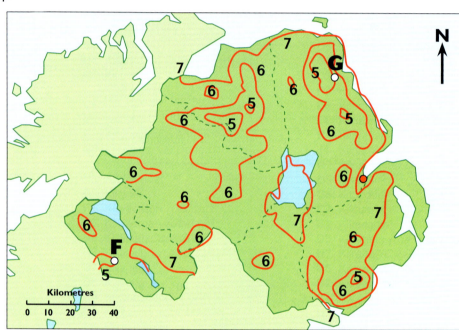

Resource N ▶

Average maximum July temperatures in °C

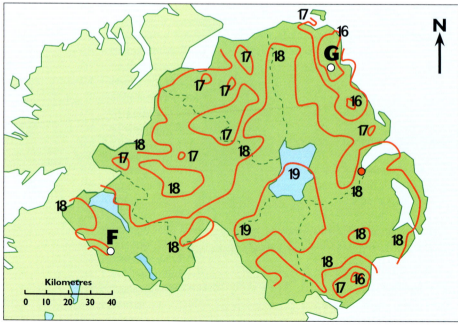

Resource O ▶

© The Met Office

Growing season

This is the number of days between the last killing frost of one winter and the first killing frost of the next winter. In Northern Ireland it can vary from 210 days in upland areas to 300 days on the east coast. The length of the growing season varies from year to year and dictates what crops the farmer can or cannot grow. In spring when temperatures stay consistently above 6°C, plants begin to grow. In autumn they stop growing once temperatures fall below 6°C for any length of time.

Average rainfall in mm

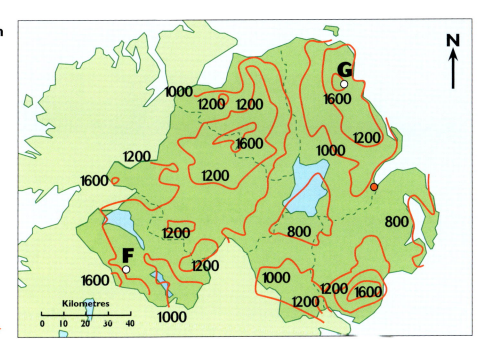

Resource P ▶

Growing season in days

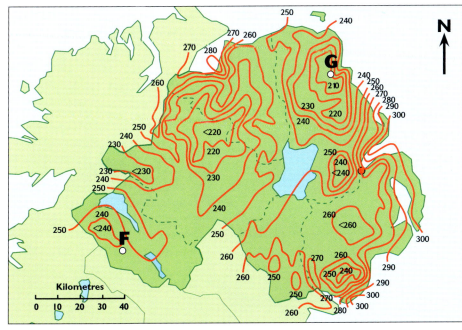

Resource Q ▶

© The Met Office

The climate statistics for the nearest weather station are as follows:

GLENARIFF

	Jan	Feb	Mar	Apr	May	Jun	Jul	Aug	Sept	Oct	Nov	Dec
Temp (°C)	2.7	2.6	3.9	5.8	8.3	11.1	12.6	12.5	10.7	8.4	4.9	3.7
PPT (mm)	183	123	148	107	100	102	103	133	154	177	186	175

Total PPT 1691 mm   Range of temperature 10.0

LISNASKEA

	Jan	Feb	Mar	Apr	May	Jun	Jul	Aug	Sept	Oct	Nov	Dec
Temp (°C)	4.1	4.3	5.8	7.7	10.3	13.2	14.8	14.4	12.5	10.0	6.4	4.9
PPT (mm)	104	73	82	53	70	66	57	86	86	103	92	100

Total PPT 973 mm   Range of temperature 10.7

© The Met Office

On the European map these areas would be shown as having the same climate, but there are important differences for the farmers concerned in temperature, rainfall and the growing season. Climate is only one of the factors which the farmer has to think about.

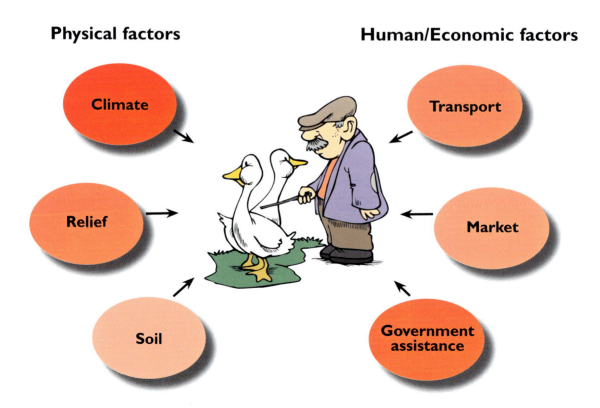

Physical factors   **Human/Economic factors**

Climate

Transport

Relief

Market

Soil

Government assistance

Resource R compares the two farms under some of these headings. This is followed by a summary of each of the two farms.

Resource R ▶

	Dieskirt Farm *James McHenry*	**Tullyhona Farm** *Geoffrey Armstrong*
Location **Nearest town** **Height above sea level**	Glenariff Ballymena 25 km 100 –350 metres	Florence Court Enniskillen 12 km 70–300 metres
Soil	Light, infertile, runs up to peat on the higher ground	Wet and heavy, only 6–7 cm of soil in places, limestone
Size	Total land area 191 ha 166 ha (includes 12.5 ha of inbye land) plus 25 ha of conacre	Total land area 360 ha 150 ha plus 210 rented
Crops	Grass 7% Rough grazing 93%	Grass 77% Rough grazing 23%

Livestock
  Dairy cattle
  Beef cattle
  Sheep
	None
	10 suckler cows and 20 calves
	200 Scottish Blackface, 300 Texel and 700 lambs
		None
		200 suckler cows and 200 calves
		50 Suffolk and 80 lambs

Labour	2	2
Main products & market	Lambs to Dungannon market for export to France, beef cattle to Saintfield Market	Beef cattle to Enniskillen and lambs to Dungannon
Diversification	Bed & Breakfast	Bed & Breakfast and a restaurant

Government/EU assistance	The link between subsidies and production has been removed. This is called **decoupling.** This means the farmer no longer needs to produce in order to receive subsidy. However, land must be kept in good agricultural and environmental condition.

- From 2005 many of the previous subsidy schemes will be replaced with a Single Farm Payment. This is made up of two parts:
  - An area component of approximately £48 per hectare
  - A historic component based on average subsidy claims in 2000–02
- Producers farming in Less Favoured Areas (LFAs) will continue to be eligible to receive the Less Favoured Area Compensatory Allowance (LFACA).
- Other payments are made to farmers who participate in agri-environment programmes, under which they agree to abide by certain conditions aimed at delivering environmental improvements, eg Countryside Management Scheme (CMS) and Environmentally Sensitive Areas (ESAs).

Dieskirt Farm – a hill farm in County Antrim

The farm
Dieskirt Farm is a ladder farm. Look at photograph A which shows the farm in the bottom of the valley with the farm running up through poor quality land to moorland grazing on the top of Glenariff – over 350 metres high. Most farms in Glenariff are laid out like this so the farmer has a share of good land, poorer land and rough grazing.

Climate
The main activity is rearing sheep and the farmer has to cope with the heavy rainfall of the area and the low winter temperatures. The minimum temperature in January, February and December is at or around freezing point. The more extreme climate of the Glenariff area means that livestock is kept indoors for 4–5 months and has to be fed on hay grown by the farmer or bought in from other farmers. Only the inbye land is suitable for growing hay; most of the 191 ha is poor quality land or moorland which does not produce much in the way of fodder.

Diversification
Even with subsidies and ESA grants the farmer has difficulty in turning a profit. The Bed & Breakfast trade is important in bringing in extra money. The farm is in the centre of the Glens of Antrim, an Area of Outstanding Natural Beauty, and is right beside Glenariff Forest Park (photograph B). The Bed & Breakfast has been expanded and trade has picked up.

Processes
The severe climate means that the 500 ewes produce only around 700 lambs per year and these are the main source of income. In July 2004, lambs were averaging £2.20 per kilo – roughly £45+ per lamb. The older ewes are sold after four or five years but do not fetch a high price. The sheep are shorn and the wool is sold but this barely covers the cost of shearing. Suckler cows will fetch more money – £800 each – but these prices are lower than they were because of BSE, and the farmer's costs have risen.

Dieskirt Farm

Labels on photograph A: Upper Glenariff Mountain — 350 m; moorland; rough grazing; inbye land

The view from Glenariff Mountain above Dieskirt Farm

The future
Farmers in the area see little future as young people are no longer willing to work a ten-hour day for 365 days per year for little or no profit. It is easier to move elsewhere or commute to a service job in a nearby settlement. The harsh climate of the area plays a part in this. There are a number of possible options for the hill farms of Glenariff and for other hill farms in Northern Ireland.
• In time the farms will be amalgamated and run by one farmer. The farmhouses may end up as second homes for people from Belfast, or sold to local people whose income is from a service industry.
• They could be bought over and managed by an **agribusiness.**
• They may simply be allowed to go back to nature.

Tullyhona Farm – a beef farm in Florence Court

The farm
The large size of this farm is due to the fact that three farms have been amalgamated into one unit. Two of the farms are beside each other and the third is 4–5 miles away. Larger farms are now more common in Northern Ireland as they find it easier to make a profit. The farm runs up to poorer rough grazing about 300 metres high (photograph B).

Suffolk sheep at Tullyhona

Climate
Despite being lower down and further west, the livestock are kept indoors for seven months of the year – from mid October to mid May. Temperatures are not high enough to enable grass to grow and the heavy rainfall means that the cattle would plough up the ground with their feet and the field could not be used for some time.

Diversification
Once again Bed & Breakfast is a useful income for the family. The farm is close to the Fermanagh Lakeland and Marble Arch Caves. Like Dieskirt Farm, the unsettled political atmosphere has cut down the number of tourists. Tullyhona is close to the border and hopes to attract visitors from the Republic of Ireland.

The highest part of the farm is on poor quality land running up to Benaughlin.

Processes
The main source of income on the farm is from the sale of 800 suckler cows every year; these fetch about £600 each. They are sold on for fattening, usually to farms further east where the climate is warmer and drier. They have to be fed indoors in winter so the main activity on the farm is the cutting and storing of silage. This is done twice a year in mid June and late August. The lambs are sold for slaughter and fetch £45 each but, like Dieskirt Farm, the ewes and the wool barely cover their costs. Before BSE, breeding cows could be sold for beef but now cows older than 30 months cannot be used for human consumption and so in many cases it costs the farmer money to dispose of them.

The future
Now that BSE is less of a problem, the beef industry is a little healthier. The large size of the farm means that it should continue to make a profit. There are still younger farmers wanting to make a living from beef. As farms amalgamate into larger units and more machinery is brought in, fewer people are needed to work the land and it is possible to make a living. Nevertheless the climate of the area means that it is difficult to diversify into other crops, so if the beef market collapses, the farmer has no other product he can turn to.

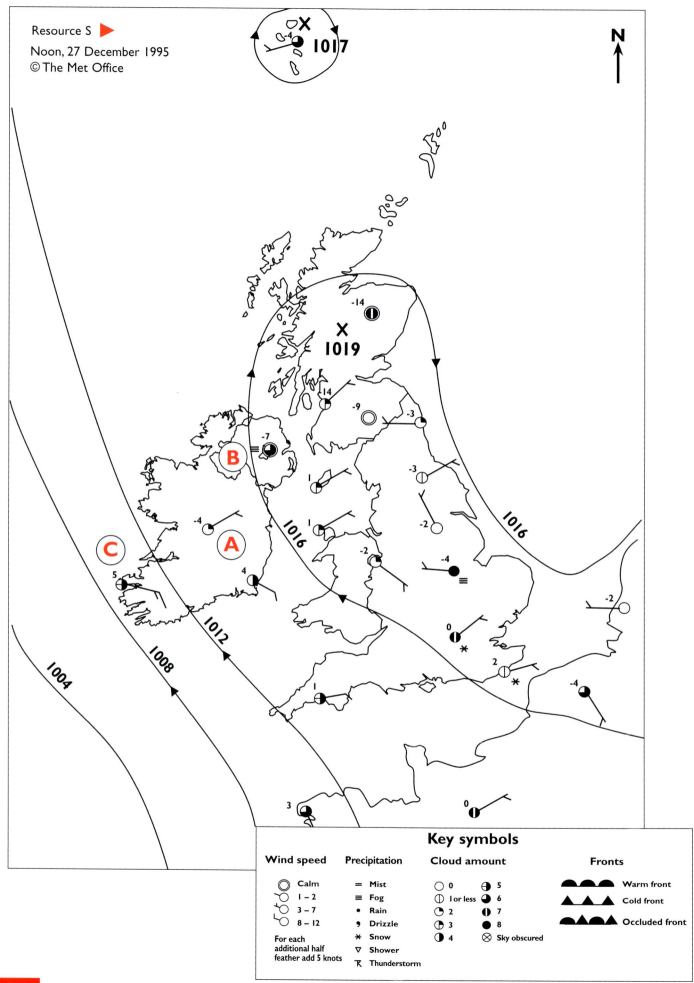

Resource S ▶

Noon, 27 December 1995

© The Met Office

N

Key symbols

Wind speed	Precipitation	Cloud amount		Fronts	
◎ Calm	≡ Mist	○ 0	◑ 5	●▲●▲● Warm front	
◐ 1 – 2	≣ Fog	◑ 1 or less	◕ 6	▲▲▲ Cold front	
◔ 3 – 7	• Rain	◔ 2	◖ 7	●▲●▲● Occluded front	
◕ 8 – 12	๖ Drizzle	◑ 3	● 8		
For each additional half feather add 5 knots	✳ Snow	◐ 4	⊗ Sky obscured		
	▽ Shower				
	𝖪 Thunderstorm				

Questions

1 Study Resource S, a synoptic chart for the British Isles, and answer the following questions. The number of marks for each question is given. Questions with one mark have a one word answer. In questions with two or three marks you would be expected to write two or three lines.

(a) Rewrite these three sentences choosing the correct word from the list given.
   (i) The map shows a depression/cyclone/anticyclone/occlusion. (1)
   (ii) The coldest temperature is in Ireland/Wales/Scotland. (1)
   (iii) There is snow in SE/SW/NW England. (1)

(b) What is the wind speed and direction at Station A? (2)

(c) Station B is based at Aldergrove Airport. State why flights leaving the airport might be delayed at this time. (2)

(d) What is the pressure at Station C? (1)

2 Study the graph in Resource T which shows weather readings taken in September/October 2000 in Bangor and answer these questions.

(a) Which day recorded the highest maximum temperature? (1)
(b) What was the highest minimum temperature? (1)
(c) What was the daily range on 27 September? (2)
(d) What was the average temperature on 6 October? (2)
(e) What was the total rainfall for 9 October? (2)

Resource T ▼

Graph of maximum–minimum temperatures plotted with rainfall 26 Sept to 16 Oct 2000

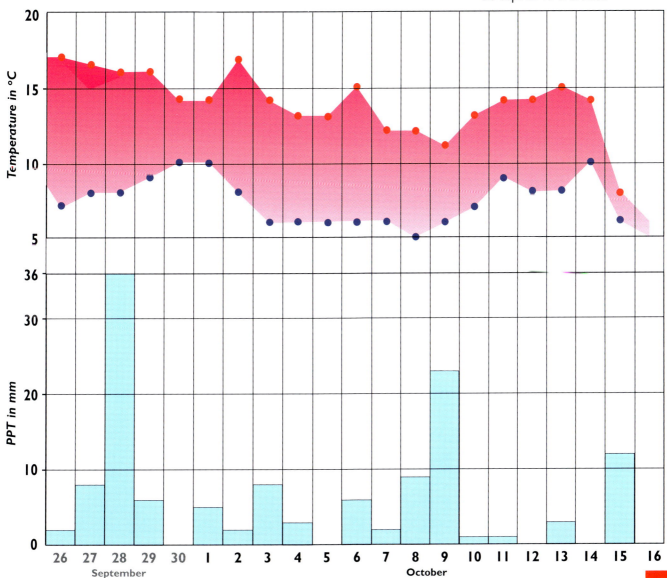

Physical Processes and Challenges

This theme concentrates on the structure of the Earth, processes which produce varying landscapes and on human responses to them, including issues relating to hazard management. Landscapes are a product of the movement of sediment across the Earth's surface, weathering and erosion processes, both past and present, and human activities.

1.3 Earthquakes

The crust of the Earth is divided into large sections called plates. The plates move slowly, driven by convection currents in the mantle. Plates do not slide smoothly past each other. They can jam and cause a build up of pressure. Eventually the pressure will become so great that the plates will move with a jerk and this is what causes a quake or a tremor. Earthquakes are measured on a scale called the Richter Scale (named after American geologist Charles Richter). The scale measures the magnitude of the earthquake and tells us how much energy is released.

The Richter Scale

1. So small they cannot be felt

2. Ponds ripple and doors sway.

3. Hanging objects swing.

4. Buildings shake as if a large lorry had passed.

5. Crockery rattles.

6. Furniture moves and walls may crack.

7. Roads shake, poor buildings fall, strong buildings are damaged.

8. Most buildings fall, roads crack, bridges collapse, pipes burst.

9. Widespread destruction

The scale is a logarithmic scale, so a 7.0 earthquake is 10 times more powerful than a quake of 6.0. An 8.0 quake is 10 times more powerful than a 7.0, and 100 times more powerful than a 6.0. Earthquakes below 6 do not usually cause deaths but may do damage to buildings. Earthquakes above 6.0 are more likely to cause deaths or do serious damage to buildings. Earthquakes themselves do not kill people. The buildings people live and work in cause the deaths. There are a number of factors which will determine the damage and number of deaths:

- The distance from the epicentre. The further away the epicentre is, the less the damage will be.

Resource A ▶

The Earth's crust showing the epicentre and focus of a quake

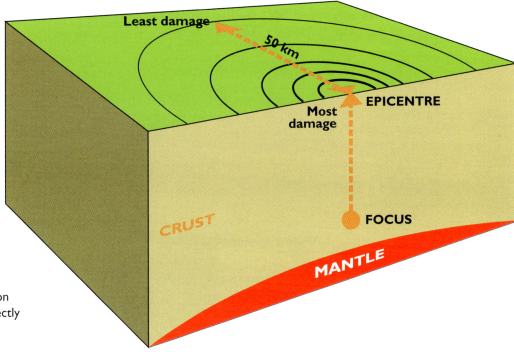

FOCUS – where the earthquake takes place

EPICENTRE – the place on the surface of the crust directly above the focus

- How deep in the Earth's crust the earthquake is. The deeper it is, the less the damage.

- The time of day. At night people will be asleep and at home. They are less likely to be in an earthquake-proof building. During the day they will be at work and are more likely to be in a safer building, but the roads and railways will have more traffic on them.

- Whether the epicentre is in a rural or an urban area. Some large earthquakes have done little or no damage as they have happened in very remote areas. Smaller earthquakes that occur in urban areas can do more damage.

- Whether a country is an MEDC (More Economically Developed Country) or an LEDC (Less Economically Developed Country). MEDCs have better building codes, better emergency services, more specialised equipment and more money. LEDCs lack all of these and this can result in higher death tolls. It is rare for survivors to be rescued more than 24 hours after an earthquake. MEDCs have the resources to mount a quick rescue effort; LEDCs do not.

- How much money has been put into earthquake proofing the buildings, bridges and roads. MEDCs can afford to do this and they have strict building regulations and controls. LEDCs do not have these, and even if they do, bribery and corruption mean that sometimes laws are ignored.

Case study   **One earthquake event in either an LEDC or an MEDC**

We will look at two earthquakes, one in an MEDC (Japan) and one which affected 12 LEDCs (South-East Asian tsunami). In both case studies there is a long history of seismic activity.

MEDC   Kobe, Japan   17 January 1995

Japan is probably the world's leading country in terms of studying and preparing for earthquakes. Japan has spent a lot of money trying to predict earthquakes and in ensuring that the country is as well prepared as possible. Earthquakes happen regularly because the Pacific Plate is sliding underneath the Eurasian Plate and Japan is on the edge of the plate boundary. Even the Japanese were surprised by the damage caused by the quake.

- The earthquake happened at 5.45 am.
- It measured 6.9 on the Richter Scale.
- It was only 22 kilometres down in the Earth's crust and the epicentre was 35 kilometres from Kobe.

Earthquake damage in Kobe

Short-term effects (what happened during the earthquake)

- 6433 dead (58% of the dead were over 60)
- 36 000 injured
- 310 000 evacuated
- Over 130 000 houses were damaged or destroyed.
- The Hanshin Expressway collapsed.
- The port was put out of action.
- City-wide power and water failure, 25% phone failure, 80% gas failure
- One-third of the shopping area damaged
- Total cost of $200 billion

Long-term effects (what happened over the months and years following the earthquake)

- 82 000 houses needed
- People who were in evacuation shelters long term (some as long as 7 years) needed help and support for depression and other mental problems.
- Schools could not function properly as they were being used for shelters and temporary accommodation.
- Long-term damage to the infrastructure
- Drastic rise in unemployment due to damaged industries having to close or relocate away from Kobe

A collapsed building in Kobe

Nearly 10 years on, Kobe has made a remarkable recovery.

- Water, gas, electric and telephones were working by July 1995.
- The railways were working by August 1995.
- 80% of the port was working within a year.
- By January 1999, 134 000 housing units had been built.

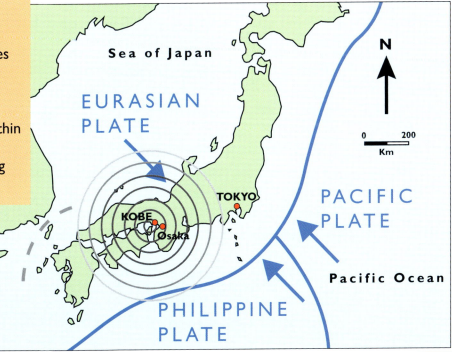

LEDC   South-East Asian tsunami   26 December 2004

This area has suffered from many earthquakes in the recent past, but does not have the resources to prepare for or cope with large earthquakes. Earthquakes happen because the Indian Plate is colliding with the Burma Plate.

- The earthquake happened at 8.30 am.
- It measured 9 on the Richter Scale.
- It was only 10 kilometres down in the Earth's crust and the epicentre was below the seabed, about 80 kilometres off the west coast of Sumatra.

DigitalGlobe

Banda Aceh, Indonesia, before the tsunami

Short-term effects (what happened during the earthquake)

- The energy released was the equivalent of 23 000 nuclear bombs being detonated at the same time.
- The earthquake lasted for 3 to 4 minutes.
- The seabed moved up to 10 metres sideways and was pushed upwards 3 to 4 metres.
- A large tsunami (Japanese for 'harbour wave') was generated in the sea at the epicentre of the earthquake. This radiated out at speed (240 kilometres per hour) from the epicentre, reaching the coast of Indonesia in 20 minutes.
- It affected 12 countries around the Indian Ocean, reaching Sri Lanka in 2 hours, and Kenya in 4 hours.
- As near as can be estimated the total death toll is as high as 300 000. This included people from over 60 countries, many of them tourists in the area.
- The number of homeless is estimated to be 1.75 million.
- The map on page 33 (Resource C) shows the damage caused around the Indian Ocean.

Long-term effects (what happened over the months following the earthquake)

- The World Food Programme was feeding 1.1 million people by the end of January 2005.
- In the 3 days after the earthquake there were 68 large aftershocks; 13 of these registered over 6 on the Richter Scale. These hampered the rescue efforts as people feared more tsunamis.

- There was a long-term impact on tourism which fell in some areas by as much as 70% in the months following the tsunami. Hotels were destroyed, bookings cancelled and jobs lost.

- Many fishermen in the area lost their boats and nets and were left with no way of earning a living.

- Governments and organisations pledged over $7 billion. Not all the aid that was pledged was actually delivered. This is a common pattern. After the earthquake in Bam in Iran on Boxing Day 2003, over $1 billion was promised, but only $115 million arrived. After Hurricane Mitch in the Caribbean in 1998, $9 billion was promised but only half ever arrived.

- Rebuilding work was slow to start. In Sri Lanka rebuilding was banned within 200 metres of the sea and this caused problems for the fishermen. At the time of writing, many people were still living in tents in refugee camps. Indonesia estimated it would take at least 5 years to fully recover. The UN (United Nations) thought the recovery would be measured in decades not years.

DigitalGlobe

Banda Aceh, Indonesia after the tsunami

Contrasts in response between an LEDC and MEDC

It is clear when you look at an earthquake that the MEDC response is better than the LEDC response. This is because the MEDC has more money, a better infrastructure and more modern equipment than an LEDC. They can put strategies into effect that will lessen the damage done by an earthquake. LEDCs do not have the money and/or technology to do all this.

- Buildings should be made earthquake resistant. In Japan skyscrapers have been built to resist earthquakes. These building techniques are expensive and they have to be enforced. In South-East Asia the simple brick, wood and thatched buildings were washed away by the power of the tsunami.

- Public buildings need to be especially secure as they will be essential for recovery after the quake, eg hospitals, schools, police stations, and fire stations. Bridges and elevated motorways can also be reinforced to minimise damage. In the LEDCs around the Indian Ocean there is no money for this.

- The government/local authority also needs a plan for the local area. Plans need to be practised and reviewed on a regular basis – at least annually.

- Emergency supplies need to be stored, preferably somewhere earthquake resistant. Supplies include dried food, water purifying tablets, tents, plastic sheeting, first aid supplies, etc.

- Specialist equipment needs to be on hand or easily available. This includes Disaster Response Teams, listening devices, infrared cameras, fibre optic cameras, and dog teams.

- Each home should have an earthquake emergency kit and a plan (see Resource B).

Resource B ▶

> - *Water and food for three days, water purification tablets, heavy-duty gloves, first aid kit, cash (ATM may be shut down), family photos (to help find missing relatives), torch, portable radio, batteries, goggles, dust mask, washbag and toilet paper, disposable barbecue, large bin-bags, and matches.*
> - *Know how to shut off water, electricity and gas.*
> - *Plan to reunite your family so as you know who is missing.*
> - *Keep a torch, slippers (broken glass on floor) and a jemmy (doors may jam) under your bed.*
> - *Keep your mobile phone off – it probably will not work anyway!*

- MEDCs have the money and technology to put all these plans into effect before the earthquake strikes. LEDCs do not have the money or the infrastructure to prepare well. They cannot afford to put these plans into operation.

- MEDCs can mobilise rescue services and the army very quickly while LEDCs cannot. Japan had helicopters and heavy machinery available in large numbers within 24 hours. In South-East Asia it took much longer for these to become available and there were fewer of them.

- The MEDCs around the Pacific Ocean have a tsunami warning system in place that can give the authorities time to evacuate people to higher ground. It was considered too expensive to put a similar system in place in the Indian Ocean.

I really feel for all these people – not just for what they have been through, but for what they still have to go through.

Compare the development levels of these countries to see which ones will respond best to a disaster caused by an earthquake.

	Indonesia	India	Thailand	Sri Lanka	Japan	USA
Total debt ($)	132 bn	105 bn	60 bn	10 bn	–	–
Debt repayment per year ($)	14 bn	13 bn	18 bn	0.7 bn	–	–
Debt as a % of income	80	21	48	59	–	–
GDP (Gross Domestic Product) ($)	817	487	2060	873	31 407	36 006
% below poverty line	27	29	13	25	0	0
HDI (Human Development Index)	111	127	76	96	9	8

Topfoto/Photri

Banda Aceh, Sumatra,
Indonesia
(1 January 2005)

Resource C ▼

N

DEAD 2
BANGLADESH

DEAD 10 000
INDIA
HOMELESS 140 000

DEAD 59
BURMA

DEAD 200
SOMALIA
HOMELESS 30 000

DEAD 8500
THAILAND

DEAD 36 000
SRI LANKA
HOMELESS 800 000

DEAD 68
MALAYSIA

DEAD 1
KENYA

DEAD 240 000
INDONESIA
HOMELESS 800 000

DEAD 100
MALDIVES
HOMELESS 12 500

DEAD 10
TANZANIA

DEAD 1
SEYCHELLES

DEAD 8000
**ANDAMAN &
NICOBAR ISLES**
HOMELESS 12 000

0   700   1400

Km

Meulaboh, Sumatra, Indonesia (10 January 2005)

Listening in Geography can save your life!

Ten-year-old Tilly Smith was on holiday with her family in the Thailand resort of Maikhao Beach. When the sea retreated down the beach Tilly remembered that this was one of the warning signs of a tsunami she had learnt about in a Geography lesson in school. She said, "Mummy, we must get off the beach now! I think there's going to be a tsunami." The adults did not understand until Tilly added the words "a tidal wave". The warning spread and over 100 people evacuated the beach. This was one of the only places near Phuket where no one was killed or seriously injured. Tilly was quick to give credit to her Geography teacher – Andrew Kearney, at Danes Hill Preparatory School, in Surrey, England.

28 March 2005

At 2315 local time a magnitude 8.7 earthquake hit the Indonesian island of Nias. The countries round the Indian Ocean issued a tsunami alert and thousands of people moved away from coastal areas. The epicentre was 30 kilometres deep and the fault moved laterally not vertically so there was no large tsunami.

Nevertheless, over 2000 people were killed on the island of Nias and many of the concrete buildings which had survived the tsunami were destroyed. Roads were impassable, the airport was out of action, and power failed.

2.1 Characteristics of a drainage basin

Northern Ireland is drained by many large rivers. The area drained by a river and its tributaries is called a drainage basin or catchment area. The boundary of a drainage basin is called the watershed.

The river will change on the way downstream from source to mouth. At the source it may be small enough to jump over, whereas at the mouth it may be very wide and deep.

We need to look at some of the changes that occur in a river from source to mouth.

Resource D ▶

Width   This is normally measured from the water's edge at one side to the water's edge at the other side (see Resource D).

Depth   This can be measured at one point or average depths can be taken across the stream (see Resource D).

Discharge   This is a measure of how much water flows down the river. It is measured in cumecs – cubic metres per second. It is calculated by measuring the width, average depth and speed of the river and multiplying them together (see Resources E and F).

If a river is 6 metres wide, has an average depth of 0.5 metres and is flowing at 2 metres per second (mps), then the discharge will be:
6 x 0.5 x 2 = 6 cumecs

This means that in one second, 6 cubic metres of water will flow past a point on the bank.

Resource E ▶

Resource F ▼

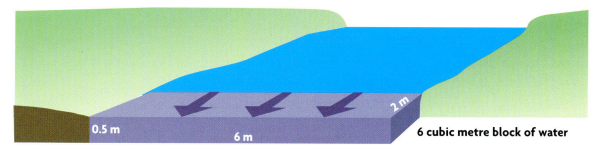

0.5 m
6 m
2 m
6 cubic metre block of water

Load   This is the material carried downstream by the river. It varies from minute particles of silt/sand that can hardly be seen to pebbles, stones and large boulders. The material that makes up the load can fall into the river or be washed out from the bed and banks.

A

Photograph A shows a bank of shingle deposited in the river bed. It has been there a long time and plants have started to grow on it. It would take an extreme flood for this material to be washed downstream.

Photographs B and C show water taken from the river during a flood. In photograph B the silt is suspended in the water and would be carried downstream. When the river loses energy the silt falls to the bed of the river. Photograph C is taken 24 hours after photograph B.

B

C

Case study   River Bann

In world terms the Bann is not a very big river. Resource G compares the Bann to the Amazon in South America.

Resource G ▶

	Bann	**Amazon**
Length	145 km (90 miles)	6577 km (4110 miles)
Drainage basin (km²)	4500	7 180 000
Discharge (cumecs)	132	180 000

Despite its small size, it is the longest river in Northern Ireland. Resource H shows the drainage basin of the Bann which drains 38% of Northern Ireland.

1	**Lower Bann**
2	**Upper Bann**
3	**Main**
4	**Moyola**
5	**Ballinderry**
6	**Blackwater**
7	**Sixmilewater**
C	**Coleraine**
K	**Kilrea**
T	**Toome**
P	**Portadown**
B	**Banbridge**
S	**Spelga**
LB	**Lough Beg**
LN	**Lough Neagh**

Resource H ▼   The drainage basin of the River Bann

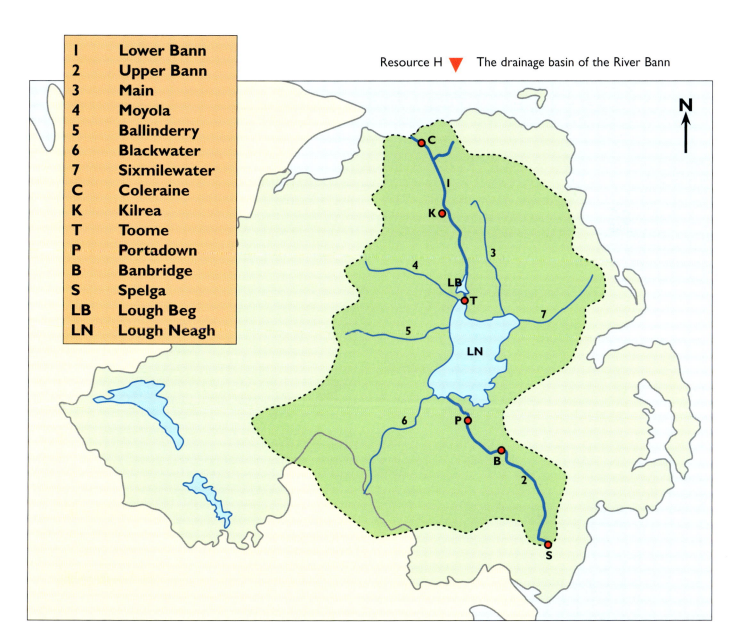

We will follow the river from source to mouth to see what changes take place.

The photograph below shows the source of the Bann in the Mourne Mountains above Spelga Dam. The Bann flows out of this wet boggy patch in the grass and starts its long journey to the sea. At this point it is impossible to measure its width and depth – it is too small.

Source of the Bann

Within 100 metres of the source the Bann flows into Spelga Dam. Water from Spelga is piped to Portadown over 50 kilometres away. This is man's first attempt to manage or control the river. The dam helps to control flooding lower down the valley. This is a good example of hard engineering, where walls and channels of concrete are used to manage the river. Below Spelga the river varies in width and depth depending on how much water has been released from the dam. If the dam is full there will be a good flow, but if the weather is dry little water will be released into the channel and the river's discharge will be much smaller.

Spelga

Below Spelga Dam the river's load is often deposited, as there may not be enough energy to carry it downstream. The photograph below shows the load of the Bann below Spelga Dam. There are many large stones and they are more angular in shape as they are near the source and have not been eroded.

The load near the source

By the time the river has reached Banbridge it has travelled 35 kilometres from the source and is much wider and deeper.

Banbridge

After travelling over 50 kilometres from the source, it flows through Portadown. Shortly afterwards it flows into Lough Neagh, the largest inland lake in the British Isles.

Portadown

Five other big rivers flow into Lough Neagh (Main, Blackwater, Moyola, Ballinderry and Sixmilewater) but only one river – the Lower Bann – drains Lough Neagh. The river leaves Lough Neagh at Toome and it is here that man's attempts to manage the river are very obvious. The photograph below shows the first of five sluices and weirs used to control water levels in the Lower Bann. The weir controls water levels in Lough Neagh, ensuring that they do not drop below a certain level. This is a further example of hard engineering.

Toome

Three kilometres downstream from Toome is Lough Beg. This is a wide shallow lough where the river can flood out over its channel. In winter when the river is high the lough is wider and deeper. In summer when the river is low the lough is much smaller and shallower and the surrounding grassland can be used by farmers to graze their cattle. This is an example of soft engineering, where the natural flooding of the river acts as a reservoir and helps prevent flooding downstream.

Lough Beg

There are very few bridges between Toome and the sea, as the river is now wider and deeper. In this stretch it is joined by the Clady River, another major tributary. At Kilrea the river is over 70 metres wide.

Kilrea

When the river finally reaches Coleraine, four more large rivers have increased the discharge in the Bann – Aghadowey, Macosquin, Agivey and Ballymoney rivers. It is now wide enough and deep enough to take sea-going ships, so a port has grown up on the east bank of the river just below the lowest bridging point in the town.

Coleraine

The final nine kilometres of the river is tidal. This means that the depth will vary according to the tide. The river finally reaches the sea at the Barmouth, and again there are good examples of hard engineering here. Two piers have been built out into the Atlantic Ocean to help stop the river silting up, and to guide ships into the mouth of the river. The river is dredged every so often to keep the channel deep. If the channel was not dredged, then the river would deposit its load here and the channel would silt up.

Barmouth – looking upstream

At the Barmouth the load of the river consists of very fine silt, sand and mud. Only the smallest material will be washed down this far. Any stones or pebbles will be small, round and smooth as they have been eroded on their way down the river.

Barmouth – looking towards the sea

Resource 1 ▼ The depth and width of the Bann at different points from source to mouth

	Point	Width (m)	Average depth	Discharge (cumecs)+
1	Source	*	*	*
2	Spelga	2	0.05	0.02
3	Banbridge	15	0.61	1.83
4	Portadown	41	2.05	16.81
5	Toome	77	2.40	55.44
6	Kilrea	78	2.50	58.50
7	Coleraine	70	4.40	92.40
8	Barmouth	110	4.00	132.00

(* = No measurements were possible due to the lack of water in the channel.)

(+ = Average speeds were 0.2 mps from points 2 to 4, and 0.3 mps from points 5 to 8.)

Resource J  The long profile of the Bann from source to mouth (numbers refer to Resource I on page 43)

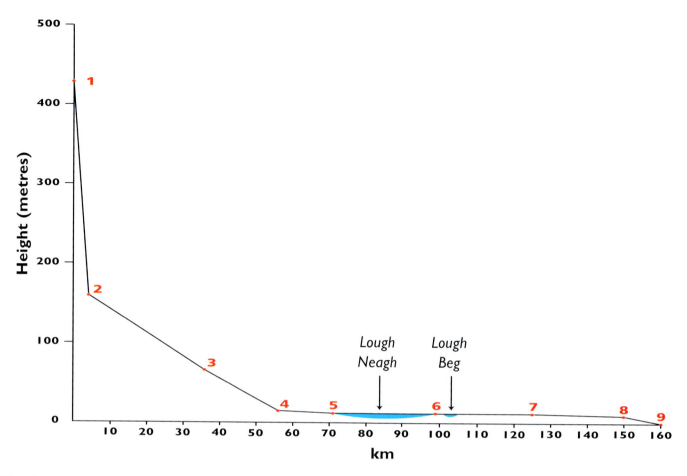

The Bann is low lying for much of its course. In the whole 60 kilometres of the Lower Bann there is only a drop of 12 metres in height.

Photographs A, B and C show how the load changes from source to mouth. As it moves downstream it becomes smaller and rounder. The lightest material travels furthest. This means that the mouth of the river has a lot of silt and sediment.

2.2 Flood hazard

Case study A river management scheme: the Strule Basin

Human activities interact with the natural processes of a river and this leads to complex management issues for the people who are looking after a drainage basin. In the case of rivers the main issue is that people want to build on flat land near the bridging point of a river and this is often where the river will flood in heavy rain. All rivers have areas which flood in heavy rain. These areas are called flood plains. Look at the photographs (Resource K) of the Callan River in County Armagh.

Resource K ▼

December 1999

April 2000

In rural areas like this the flood plain is not built on and the river can flood without causing too much damage. They may be dry for several years or they may flood annually. Flood plains are usually flat, fertile areas, so they are attractive to humans for settlement. Many of the world's largest cities are built on flood plains, as are many towns in Ireland. We will look at a case study from Omagh to see what the problem is, what groups are involved and what decision has been taken.

The problem

Omagh is a bridging point and route centre at the confluence of the Camowen and Drumragh Rivers. These rivers join and form the River Strule. Four kilometres further downstream, the Fairy Water also joins the Strule.

The drainage basin of the Strule and the Fairy Water covers nearly 750 square kilometres (see Resource L). Both these rivers are part of the Foyle Basin and eventually drain into Lough Foyle at Derry. The Foyle drainage basin covers over 2800 square kilometres of Northern Ireland and extends into the Republic of Ireland as well.

Resource L ▶
The River Strule drainage basin

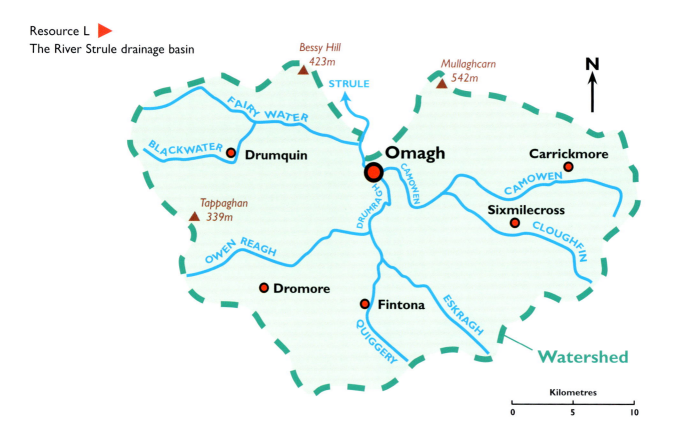

Omagh has a history of flooding and suffered major flooding in 1909, 1929, 1954 and 1969. As a result of this, floodwalls were built to keep the water in the channel and prevent it from overflowing into the flood plain. Resource M shows how engineers work out how much water the river can carry and how high the floodwalls need to be.

River Strule, looking towards Drumragh Bridge

Resource M ▼

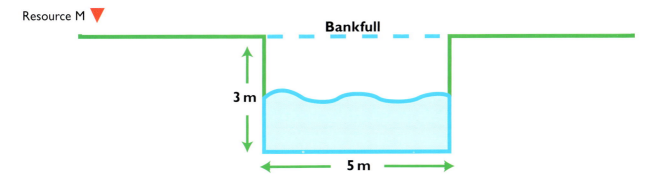

Stage 1: They work out the cross-sectional area of the river at bankfull by multiplying width and average depth. Then they multiply this by the speed of the water flowing in the river (say two metres per second) to get the discharge in cumecs (cubic metres per second). This is the bankfull capacity of the river. If the discharge is greater than 30 cumecs then the river will overflow its banks.

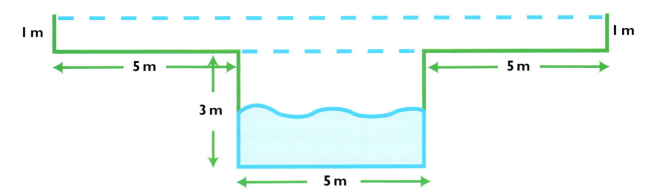

Stage 2: If a wall is built one metre high five metres from each bank, this increases the amount of water that the river can carry. If the discharge is greater than 60 cumecs then the river will overflow the floodwall.

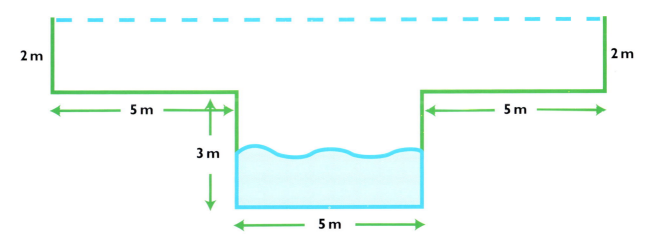

Stage 3: If height of the wall is increased to two metres, the river can carry 90 cumecs before the river will overflow the floodwall. If the speed is greater than two metres per second, the river will carry more water. This is an example of hard engineering.

On Wednesday 21 October 1987, there was a period of prolonged heavy rain (57 mm in 22 hours). The ground in the drainage basin was already saturated from earlier rain, so most of this water ran off into the rivers which quickly became swollen.

The problem started on the afternoon of Wednesday 21 October when traders and residents in the Campsie area realised that the rivers were rising quickly. By 7.00 pm the water had backed up into the drains and sewers and water was flooding up through the gratings and manholes. By midnight the Drumragh, Camowen and Strule Rivers had reached the top of the existing flood barriers, and shortly after 4.00 am on 22 October the water flooded over the floodwalls into the town. The photographs (Resources N, O, P, Q, R, S and T) show the extent of the flooding on the morning of Thursday 22 October.

Resource N ▼

Esler Crawford Photography

Omagh looking north over the Drumragh/Camowen confluence

1	**Drumragh River**	7	**Secondary School playing fields**
2	**Camowen River**	8	**Leisure Centre**
3	**Confluence**	9	**Campsie Crescent**
4	**River Strule**	10	**Joe Mahon's butchers shop**
5	**Omagh County Primary School**	11	**Francey O'Neill's Home Décor Centre**
6	**Campsie Road**	12	**King James' Bridge**

Esler Crawford Photography

Omagh looking upstream towards the south-east

1	**River Strule**	4	**Gortmore Gardens**	7	**Derry Road**
2	**Sewage Works**	5	**Strathroy Estate**	8	**Town centre**
3	**Hunter Crescent**	6	**Watson Park**		

Resource P ▼

Campsie Road under water, 22 October 1987

Resource Q ▼

Campsie Road was the worst hit. Campsie Crescent flooded by 7.00 pm and the water eventually rose to a height of two metres. Seventy residents were rescued by army boats during the night. Two hundred premises were flooded and tens of thousands of pounds worth of stock and equipment were destroyed. Many residents were marooned in their houses and were brought food by the emergency services.

Resource R ▼

Camowen River behind Campsie Road

This scene is eight hours after the flood peaked and the river is still running high.

Resource S ▼

Omagh County Primary School was flooded to a depth of 0.6 metres and had to close for two weeks. It suffered £100 000 worth of damage, mainly to floors and electrics.

Resource T ▼

King James' Bridge on the Irishtown Road remained impassable the following morning.

The groups involved

The main people involved were the unfortunate residents of Campsie, Hunter Crescent and Gortmore Gardens.

The McMahon family were evacuated from their house in Campsie Crescent by the army. The area flooded to a depth of two metres. Their butcher's shop on Campsie Road was flooded to a depth of 0.7 metres and their store in Campsie Crescent was flooded to a depth of 1.5 metres. It was over two weeks before they were back in business as they had lost thousands of pounds worth of stock, three vehicles, and all their equipment had been destroyed.

Resource U ▲   Joe McMahon

The Home Décor Centre actually lifted off its foundations with the force of the water and eventually was completely rebuilt. It was three days before they were able to get in to assess the damage and Mr O'Neill was out of business for two weeks. Like many of the other traders in the area, he lost thousands of pounds worth of stock. Like the McMahon family, he lived in the Campsie area and his house was flooded as well. The basement of the shop was well below the level of the Drumragh River when it was in flood. Water was forced back up the drains and sewers and overflowed in the yard and basement on the Wednesday evening, before the water breached the flood defences later that night.

Resource V ▲   Francey O'Neill

Residents in Hunter Crescent were faced with a one metre flood and evacuation by boat. They had to be rehoused while their houses were dried out. Gortmore Gardens was flooded to a depth of 0.5 metres and residents were out of their houses for between two and three months. The main repair work involved replastering the ground floor walls, lifting and relaying the floors, and checking or rewiring the electrics.

Resource W ▶

Gortmore Gardens (July 2000) with the new flood wall in place

The decision

In 1989 the Rivers Agency decided to put in place a flood alleviation scheme. It was costed at £2.4 million, was started in July 1992 and was completed in March 1993 at a cost of £2.2 million. It involved building further flood defence barriers which increased the capacity of the river. Gauging stations on the Drumragh and the Camowen will be used to ensure that adequate warning is given in the event of a serious flood problem.

The defences for Omagh were built to withstand a 100-year flood. This means that the river will overtop the floodwalls on average once every hundred years. It is possible to build higher defences but this would be more expensive. By designing to a 100-year flood, the benefits gained exceeded the cost of the works.

The figures for the Camowen River are as follows:

Resource X ▼

Year flood	Discharge
2	66 cumecs
10	85 cumecs
25	95 cumecs
50	120 cumecs
100	134 cumecs

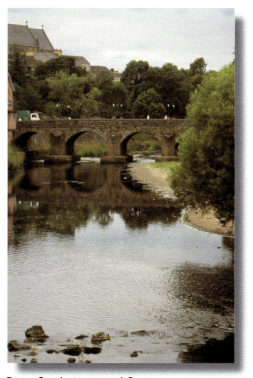

River Strule in normal flow, July 2000

River Strule in flood, October 1987

Irishtown Road in flood, October 1987

Irishtown Road two days after flood, October 1987

The current defences on the River Camowen will cope with 134 cumecs of water and on average this will be exceeded only every 100 years. If the scheme had been built to take 66 cumecs, then it would have flooded every 2 years. The Rivers Agency also looked at other ways of controlling the river. Dredging and deepening the channel can be used, but this has a bad effect on the environment and habitat of the river. Reservoirs can be built further upstream to dam the flood water, but there was no suitable site in the drainage basin of the Strule.

Resource Y

New flood defences at King James' Bridge

New flood wall at Hunter Crescent

Flood defences on the Drumragh River. The pump can be seen clearly crossing the flood defences.

Flood wall at the confluence of the Drumragh and Camowen Rivers, with Campsie Crescent behind

Residents were put on alert in December 1991 and January 1992 and many of them moved their possessions to the first floors of their houses. Fortunately no flooding occurred but in December 1999 there was further flooding caused by heavy rain in the Campsie area not being able to get into the river because of the floodwalls! The storm water in the drainage system would normally discharge into the river, but because the river was flooded it had nowhere to go except back up the drains and into the basements of the shops on Campsie Road and the gardens of Campsie Crescent. Many of the traders who suffered in 1987 were flooded again. The Home Décor Centre had 0.6 metres of water in the basement. By autumn 2000 the Water Service had installed two pumps capable of lifting the storm water into the river to overcome this problem. One of these can be seen in the bottom left photograph. Since then there have been no further problems.

3.1 Role of rock, structure and weathering process in creating the distinctive environment

The Earth's crust is composed of many different types of rock. Rocks are divided into three main types. Each type contains many different rocks.

Three types of rock

All rocks can be divided into three types depending on how they are formed.

Basalt

Chalk

Schist

IGNEOUS

The first type of rock is called igneous rock. These are 'fire-made' rocks formed from magma which has reached the surface of the Earth. The Earth's crust is not all one piece; it is divided into sections or plates like a giant jigsaw. Sometimes magma comes up to the surface between the plates and flows over the surface from a volcano or lava flow. When the magma cools it forms new rock. The main igneous rocks found in Northern Ireland are **basalt**, **granite** and **dolerite**.

SEDIMENTARY

The second type of rock is called sedimentary rock. These are 'layered' rocks formed from other rocks which have been eroded and weathered by rain, rivers and seas, and then transported and deposited under the sea. Over time they sink into the crust and form new rock. The main sedimentary rocks found in Northern Ireland are **chalk, limestone, clay, shale, greywacke** and **sandstone**.

METAMORPHIC

The third type of rock is called metamorphic rock. These are 'changed' rocks, which started off as igneous or sedimentary rocks but have been changed by being partly melted again. This happens either because they are close to a volcano or because they sink through the crust close to the mantle. The main metamorphic rocks in Northern Ireland are **schist** and **gneiss** (pronounced *nice*).

Granite

Limestone

Gneiss

3.2 Features of massive limestone environments

Rain
"It rained and it rained and rained and rained, The average fall was well maintained, And when the tracks were simply bogs, It started raining cats and dogs.

After a drought of half an hour, We had a most refreshing shower, And then the most curious thing of all, A gentle rain began to fall.

Next day was also fairly dry, Save for the deluge from the sky, Which wetted the party to the skin, And after that the rain set in."

Anonymous

Case study

Limestone features in County Fermanagh and County Clare

Limestone is a sedimentary rock. It is composed of the remains of tiny sea creatures who lived and died over 300 million years ago. Their remains piled up on the seabed and were then buried and compressed to form a rock which is at least 50% calcium carbonate.

Rainwater passing through the atmosphere picks up small amounts of carbon dioxide, turning it into a very dilute acid. More carbon dioxide is dissolved as the rain percolates through the soil and the acid becomes stronger. This reacts with the calcium carbonate making it soluble.

Limestone areas have many features which are not found in other rocks because rainwater and rivers are able to remove the limestone in solution.

Limestone is also a well jointed rock so the joints are opened up by rain and rivers. This gives a particular type of scenery called karst (after the area in Yugoslavia where it was first studied).

Resource Z ▼

We are going to concentrate on two limestone areas which are marked on the map (Resource Z) – the Marble Arch area of County Fermanagh and the Burren area in County Clare.

Limestone features

The main difference between limestone and other rocks is that in limestone areas there is very little surface drainage. The rivers dissolve the rock and work their way underground, reappearing several miles from where they go underground. There are two different types of features in limestone – surface features and underground features. Resources AA and BB show some of these features.

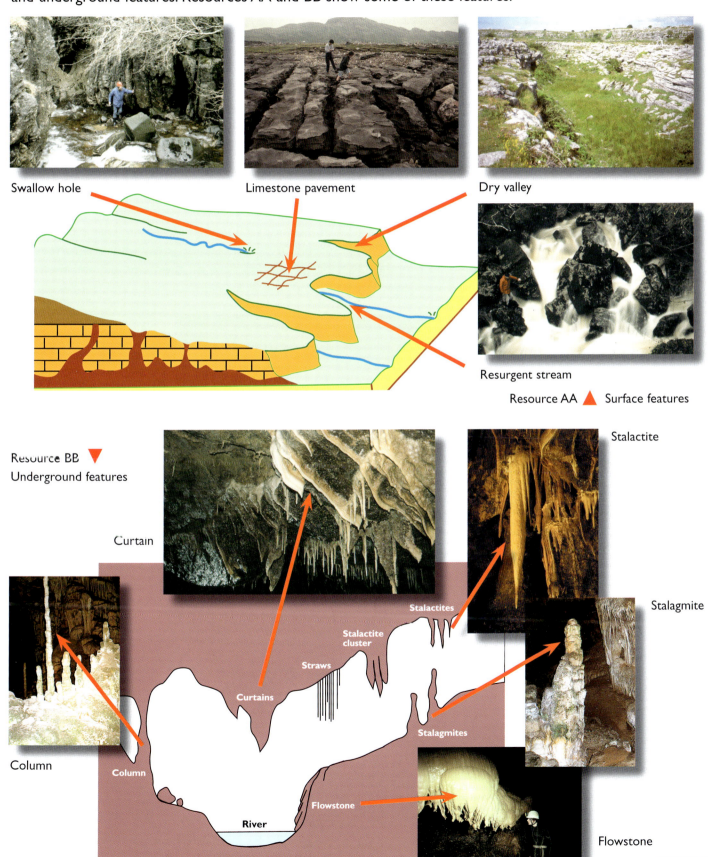

Swallow hole

Limestone pavement

Dry valley

Resurgent stream

Resource AA ▲ Surface features

Resource BB ▼
Underground features

Curtain

Column

Stalactite

Stalagmite

Flowstone

Marble Arch and the Burren both have many of these features and this has given rise to particular problems. Human activities interact with the natural processes and this leads to complex management issues for the people who are looking after the area. The areas must be managed to avoid long-term damage.

Different groups of people want different things for the area so social, economic and environmental demands can lead to different consequences. Interested groups of people want what is best for their group and may not agree with the ideas of other groups. Someone – usually the government – has to make decisions, and whatever decision is made will not please everyone. Once a decision has been made there will be winners and losers. We will look at three case studies from these limestone areas to see what the problem is, what groups are involved, what decision has been taken, and who are the winners and losers.

3.3 Human pressure in limestone environments

Case study   Peat extraction in County Fermanagh

The problem

In the late 1980s commercial peat-cutting was started on the slopes of Cuilcagh Mountain. This is the drainage basin of the Cladagh river which flows through Marble Arch Caves. The Cladagh River is formed by three smaller rivers – Sruh Croppa, Aghinrawn and Owenbrean – which flow off the mountain and then join up underground to form the Cladagh River. Resource CC shows the area, the rock types and the rivers.

Resource CC ▶

Geology of
Cuilcagh Mountain

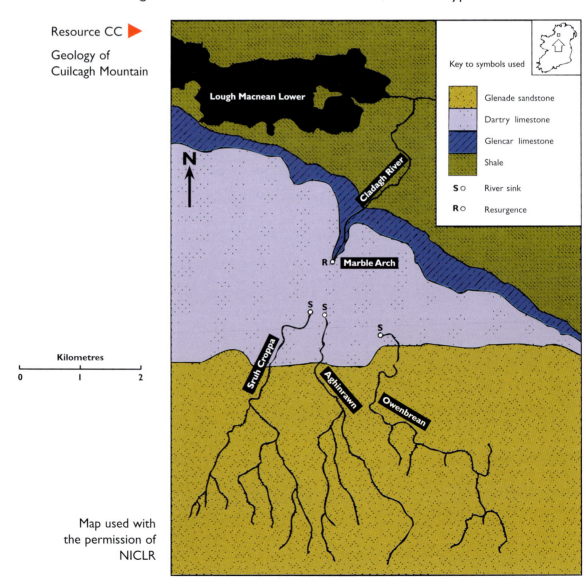

Map used with
the permission of
NICLR

During the 1990s it was noticed that the Marble Arch cave system was being flooded more often and by heavier floods. When the caves flooded they had to be closed. This led to a loss of tourist income as the caves were very popular with tourists who could explore them by boat and on foot. It was thought that mechanised peat-cutting on the mountain might be contributing to the increased flooding and that an increase in cutting might threaten the caves as a tourist attraction. Resource DD shows the increase in run off in an area where peat has not been cut compared to an area where peat has been cut.

Resource DD ▶

A **hydrograph** is a graph which plots the discharge of a river against time.

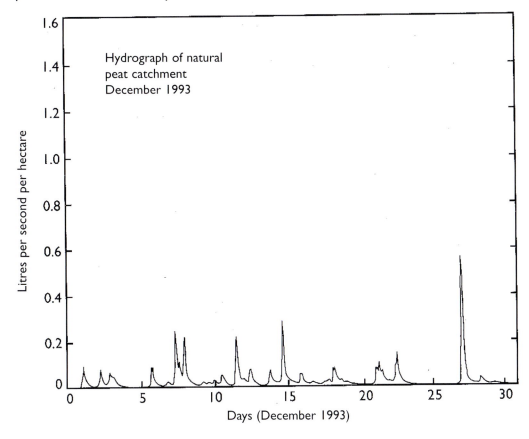

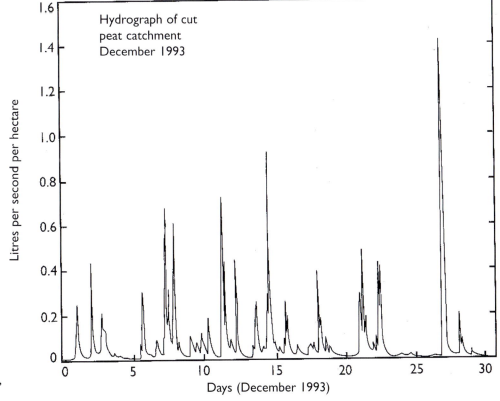

Reproduced with the kind permission of Professor John Gunn, Limestone Research Group, Geographical Sciences, University of Huddersfield

The groups involved

Farmers

We receive income from the peat cutting. We live in a Less Favoured Area (LFA) where farming is difficult and the extra income is welcome.

Fermanagh District Council

We have put a lot of time and money into the development of the cave system as a tourist attraction and we do not want to see the money wasted by having to close the caves.

The environmentalists

Northern Ireland has exploited 90% of its bogland. Bogs are rare habitats throughout the world. It has a unique environment which cannot be replaced. We are afraid that continued peat cutting will damage the area so that it can never be restored.

Moorland on Cuilcagh Mountain. The drainage channel has been dammed to try to reduce the run off.

Peat contractors

There is a market for peat and as existing sources are used up we need to find and exploit new sources. Only a small part of the mountain can be cut and we are not doing any harm.

School leaver

Tourism is bringing in jobs and money to the county and as secondary and primary jobs are harder to find, jobs in tourism may help me to stay in the area and not have to move out to look for work.

Tullyhona Farm Bed & Breakfast

I make money from tourists who may not come if the caves have to close (see page 21).

The decision

The arguments are summed up in Resource EE.

Resource EE ▶

Continue peat cutting	Stop peat cutting
• Farmers will be able to make a living in the area.	• Less water will run through the caves and they will be open more often.
• Some jobs are available cutting and processing peat.	• Tourism is more important to the local economy than farming.
• The farmers own the land and they can do what they like with it.	• We need to preserve what few bogs we have left.
• It is only a bog; it is neither valuable nor useful.	• How can we ask the Brazilians to save their tropical forest if we cannot even save our own peat bogs?
• Gardeners want peat and they might as well buy it from us.	• Some of the plants and animals are found only on peat and cannot survive anywhere else.
• If we don't cut this peat, we will only have to cut peat somewhere else.	

Before you decide on your solution to this problem, you might like to look at pages 72–77 where more information is given on peat in Northern Ireland. Once you have discussed and decided on the issue, you will find the authority's decision on page 107.

Case study   **Building an interpretive centre in the Burren, County Clare**

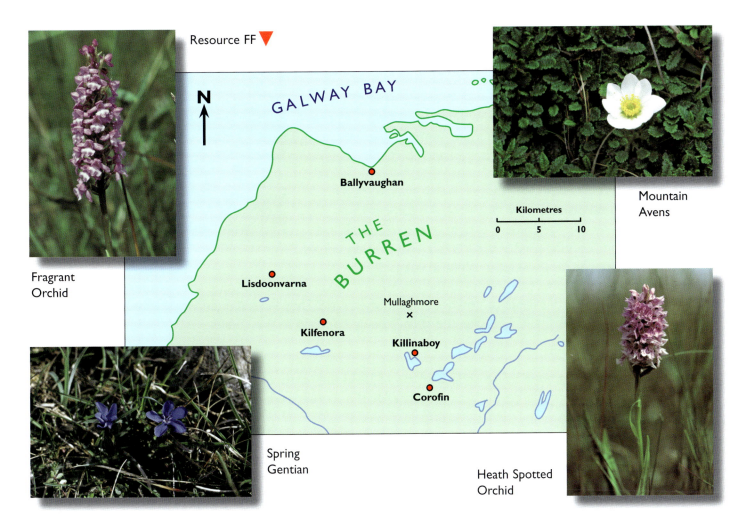

Resource FF ▼

Fragrant Orchid

Mountain Avens

Spring Gentian

Heath Spotted Orchid

The problem

The Burren is an area of over 500 square kilometres of karstic limestone in north-west County Clare which attracts over 35 000 tourists every year. It is the largest area of karstic limestone in western Europe. The tourists need to have the landscape of the area explained to them in a centre where they can look at videos, photographs, exhibitions and books. This is called an interpretive centre because it interprets the area for the tourists and helps them to understand the area before they go to look at it. There was an argument between the Office of Public Works (OPW), who wanted to build one big centre in the middle of the Burren at Mullaghmore, and some local people who wanted three smaller centres at the 'gateway villages' of Kilfenora, Corofin and Ballyvaughan on the edge of the Burren. See Resource FF.

Mullaghmore – the heart of the Burren

The groups involved

Office of Public Works (OPW)
We would like to build a centre in the Burren National Park at Mullaghmore so that tourists can learn about the area. This would bring jobs and money to the area. It will cost £2.7 million but the scheme will attract 75% grants from the EU, so it will not cost the taxpayer very much.

Kilfenora Centre
There is no need to build a new centre as there is already one here, owned and run by the local community. It provides valuable income for local people. It would be more sensible to build two smaller centres on the edge of the Burren and to spend money on the centre at Kilfenora.

The Interpretive Centre at Kilfenora

Burren Action Group
The site chosen by the government is right in the middle of the most remote and beautiful part of the Burren. They will do untold damage to the area as they will have to put in roads, sewage, electricity and water. Many of the plants in the Burren are found only here. Arctic and Mediterranean plants thrive in the same area; this happens nowhere else in the world. They have started work without planning permission (photographs B and C), while the case is being opposed in the courts.

Local contractors
We are all for this as we hope to get the contracts to build the roads, car parks and the centre itself. It will mean a lot of money coming into the area in wages for the workers we employ.

Car park at Mullaghmore (2000)

Foundations for the Interpretive Centre

Farmers
It is difficult to make much of a living in this area and we may be able to bring in extra money from increased tourism through craft shops and accommodation.

Clare County Council
We are against this scheme as the centre makes it too easy for tourists to come to the area, visit the centre, and travel on without actually seeing the Burren. They will not spend much money in the local shops or use the local services.

Turlough (disappearing lake) in the Burren

School leaver

I am not sure if the centre will provide all that many jobs once it has been built. It might be better to spread the jobs out in smaller centres away from the most beautiful and unspoilt area.

Local villagers

It will be good to have wider roads and better services but we don't want the increased traffic going through the village as it will be noisier, more polluted, and there will be an increased risk of accidents to the children. There is talk of the council having to take all the sewage away in lorries as there is nowhere to treat it in the area – that does not sound like a very sensible idea!

This typically narrow road in the Burren would have to be widened to accommodate coaches.

The decision

The arguments are summed up in Resource GG.

Resource GG ▶

Those who want to build the centre

- Local people who see a future in the jobs and money it will provide
- Farmers who may be able to make a living in the area
- Contractors who will secure jobs for the future.
- Local people who can provide services for the tourists
- The OPW who will lose the EU money if the centre is not built

Those who don't want to build the centre

- Local people who want to see the area remain unspoilt and wild
- People who think that ecotourism is more important to the local economy than mass tourism
- People who want to preserve the Burren for future generations
- Ecologists who argue that some of the plants and animals are found only in the Burren and are not found anywhere else in Ireland

Once you have discussed and decided on the issue, you will find the authority's decision on page 107.

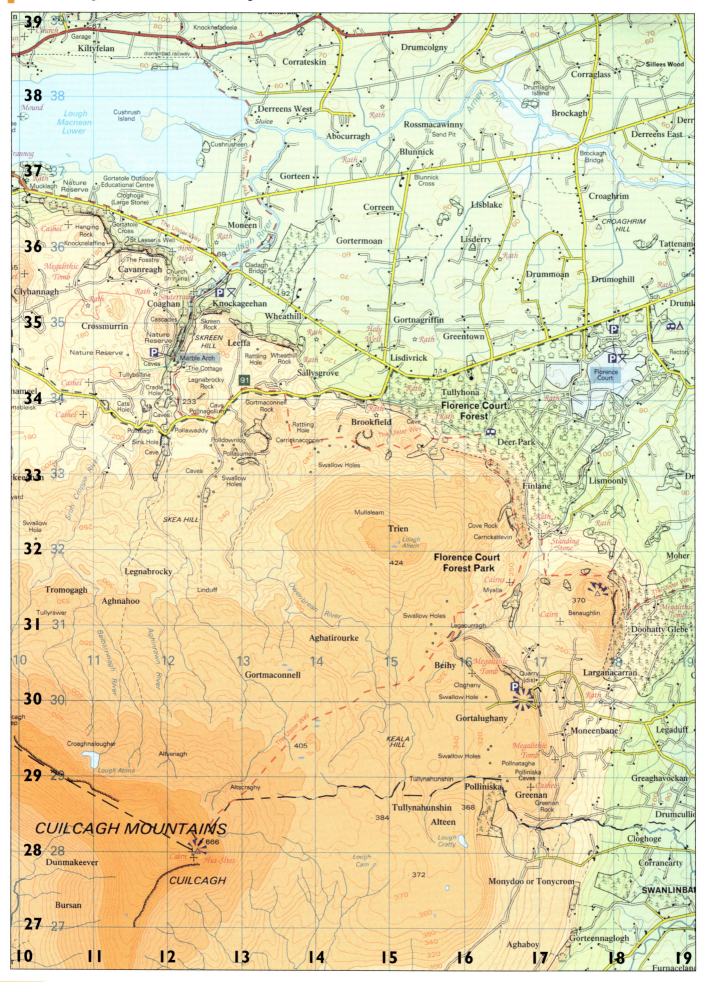

Key to Ordnance Survey map

Roads and railways

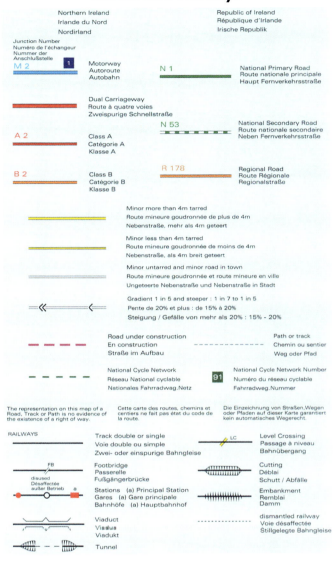

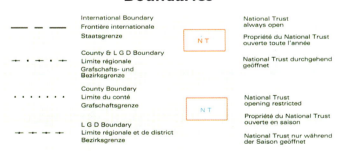

Boundaries

Location of Ordnance Survey map extract

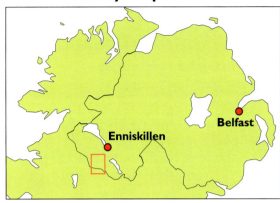

General features

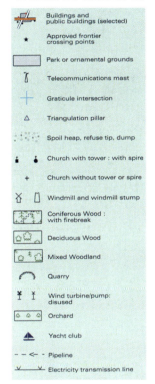

Tourist information

Antiquities

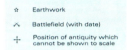

Relief

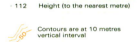

Altitudes are given in metres above Mean Sea Level at Malin Head, Co Donegal.

Water features

Abbreviations

CH	Club House
P	Post Office
PC	Public Toilets
PH	Public House
TH	Town Hall

Scale

1:50 000

2 cm to 1 km (one grid square)

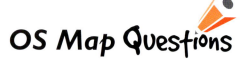

OS Map Questions

Refer to the map on page 64 and answer these questions.

1 Four figure grid references
(a) Name the island in square 1137.
(b) Name the river in square 1437.
(c) Name the tourist feature in square 1734.
(d) Name the hill in square 1232.
(e) What is the spot height in square 1534?
(f) What is the red dashed line in square 1530?

2 Six-figure grid references
What feature is found at the following grid references?
(a) 102322   (c) 149347   (e) 145372
(b) 151321   (d) 139295   (f) 110293

3 Give a six-figure grid reference for the following:
(a) Florence Court Forest Caravan Park
(b) The summit of Cuilcagh Mountain
(c) The northern point of Cushrush Island
(d) The mound in Lough Macnean Lower
(e) The cashel in square 1033
(f) The picnic site at Cladagh Bridge

4 Compass directions
In what directions are the following townlands from Sallysgrove (140343)?
(a) Corrateskin (1338)   (c) Lisblake (1636)   (e) Florence Court (1734)
(b) Cavanreagh (1135)   (d) Tromogagh (1031)   (f) Beihy (1530)

5 Scale
Measure the straight-line distance in km from Blunnick Cross junction (153370) to the following points:
(a) Y junction at Gortacole Cross (115364)
(b) Brockagh Bridge (175374)
(c) T junction (149345)

6 Photographs
Match the photographs A–H to the following grid references:
(a) 161344   (d) 165345   (g) 175343
(b) 180373   (e) 121346   (h) 186354
(c) 125376   (f) 112332

Questions

1 Study Resource HH, a newspaper report of the Omagh flood, and answer the following questions. The number of marks for each question is given. Questions with one mark have a one word answer. In questions with two or three marks you would be expected to write two or three lines.

▼ Resource HH

Saturday 24th October 1987

Drama in Omagh Floods

Our reporters found that the Campsie area was not the only part of Omagh affected by Thursday's flooding. At the Tyrone and Fermanagh Hospital over 300 patients were evacuated from the low lying Riverside Villas to the main hospital. The 700 metre walk became a 4 km detour as the Camowen River rose by 4 metres, cutting off the footbridge linking the

two areas, and threatening to flood the villas. Fortunately the villas were not flooded and the patients were able to move back on Thursday. The Nestlé factory 4 km outside the town was threatened by the Strule and the Fairy Water which surround it on two sides. Workers fought a seven hour battle from 8.30 pm, moving stock and equipment and trying to hold

back the waters with sandbags, but eventually the factory was flooded by 0.6 metres of water. The flood has caused severe disruption to the plant, causing over £1million worth of damage to powdered milk stocks and machinery. The factory may not be fully operational until the new year but it is hoped that no jobs will be lost.

(a) What was the date of the flood? (1)
(b) How many patients were evacuated from the hospital? (1)
(c) Outline two ways the factory was affected by the flooding. (2)
(d) At what time did the flood waters finally flood the factory? (2)

▼ Resource II

Esler Crawford Photography

2   Study Resource II and answer the following questions.

(a) Complete the table by adding the letters from the photograph to the correct feature.

A

River Strule	---
Bus station	---
Playing fields	---
Farmland	---
Bridge	---
Central Business District (CBD)	---
New housing estate	--- (7)

(b) The areas marked Z on the photograph have never been built over. State and explain one reason why not.

(3)

3   Study the photographs A and B which were taken in the drainage basin of the Cladagh River on the upper slopes of Cuilcagh Mountain. Answer the following questions.

B

(a) The main vegetation in photograph A is heather/grass/trees/bushes. Rewrite the sentence with the correct answer.

(1)

(b) Photograph A shows the ditches cut by the peat contractors. Why have these ditches been cut? Choose your answer from the following list:

They are to enable the cutting machines to reach the site.
They are testing the peat to see if it is deep enough to cut.
They help the water drain off so that the peat dries out.
They are paths for the workers to reach the peat cutting area.

(1)

(c) Photograph B shows the restoration work being done by the council. State and explain one difference from the area shown in photograph A.

(3)

C

4   Study photograph C which shows limestone features from Reyfad Cave, County Fermanagh.
Complete the table by adding the numbers from the photograph to the correct feature.

Stalactite	---
Stalagmite	---
Column	---
Straws	--- (4)

THEME C

Ecosystems and Sustainability

This theme concentrates on the characteristics of ecosystems and the links between the elements. Positive and negative impacts of people on ecosystems in relation to sustainability are examined.

What is an ecosystem? An ecosystem is a community and its environment working together. It includes the weather, climate, soil, animals and plants in an area (see Resource A). All ecosystems are powered by the sun which provides all the energy needed. Northern Ireland has a wide variety of ecosystems including rivers, cliffs, farmland, bogs and woodland. All of these ecosystems have a different community of flora and fauna which exist there. The climate and weather may be different in each ecosystem and land-based ecosystems may have different soils.

Resource A ▶

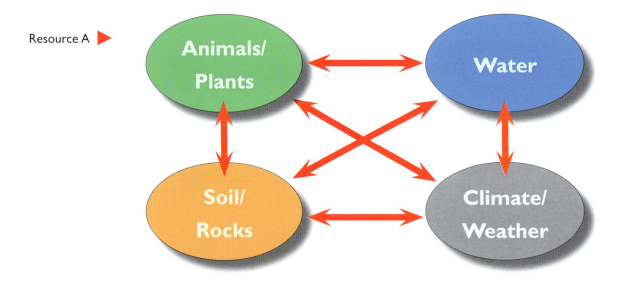

1.1 Location and distribution of ecosystems at a local scale

Northern Ireland has a number of ecosystems where the soil, climate, rocks, plants and animals interact. At one stage Northern Ireland was covered with temperate deciduous woodland like the rest of western Europe. Deciduous trees drop their leaves in autumn in order to survive the colder temperatures of winter. The woodland consisted of trees such as oak, scots pine, hawthorn, alder, willow, birch and rowan. The only areas that were not forested were high mountains, lake shores, bogs and sand dunes.

Over the last 2000 years man has gradually cut the woodland down to clear land for farming. The trees were also used for fuel and building. There are very few areas of natural woodland left. Only about 6% of Northern Ireland is still wooded and the rest has been cut down – usually for farmland. The graph on the next page shows the amount of woodland remaining in a selection of European countries.

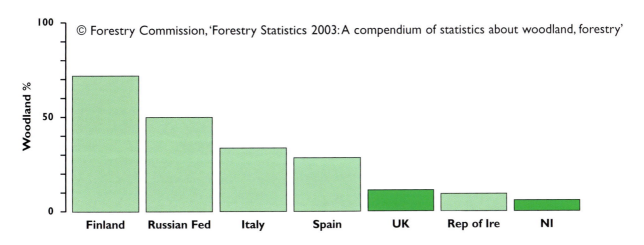

© Forestry Commission, 'Forestry Statistics 2003: A compendium of statistics about woodland, forestry'

Many of the woodland areas in Northern Ireland have been replanted. They may look old but they are not natural and have only been there for the last few hundred years or so. Many 'evergreens' have been introduced by man and are not native to Northern Ireland. This means that large areas of Northern Ireland's ecosystem are not natural but have been greatly changed by man. Man has altered all our farmland, many of our lakes have been drained and farmed on, and most of our forest parks have been planted since 1950.

Resource B shows some of our oldest remaining deciduous woodland areas. These woodlands have their own unique ecosystem with a range of plants, birds, animals and insects that interact with the local soil and climate.

Resource B ▶

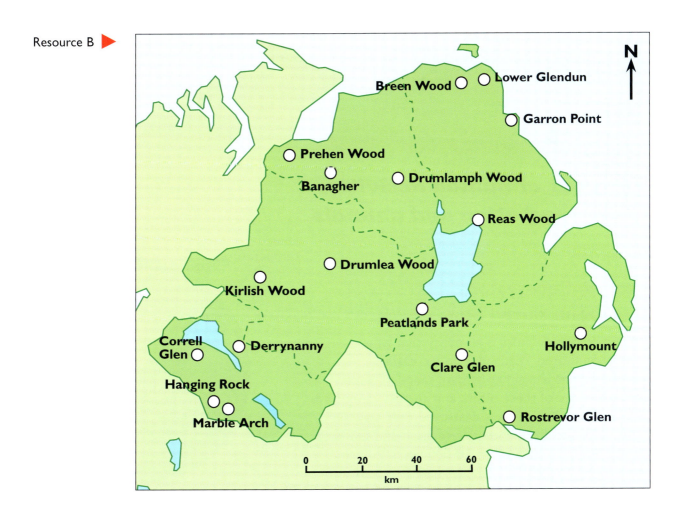

All ecosystems contain food chains or food webs. All food webs are powered by the sun which provides the energy for plants to grow. The plants are eaten by primary consumers which in turn are eaten by secondary consumers. Food webs are very complicated and easily upset by human interference.

Resource C ▼

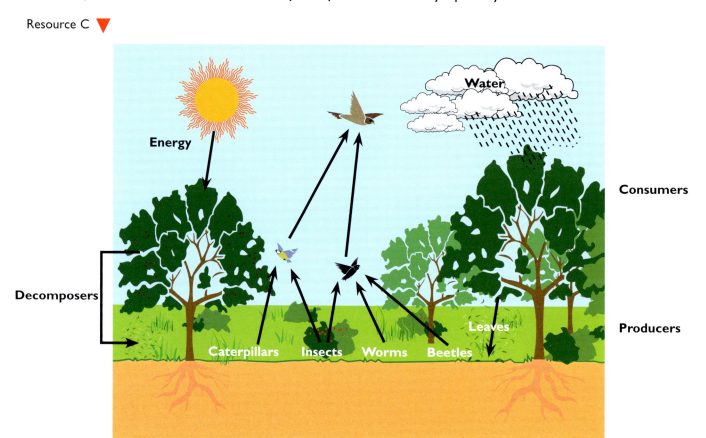

2.1 Impact of human activities on soil, vegetation and animals

Case study

A peatland ecosystem: Ballynahone raised bog

A peatland or bog or moss is an ecosystem where peat has accumulated. Peatland is an increasingly threatened habitat which has its own range of plants and animals. Some of these plants and animals cannot live anywhere else so if the bog is destroyed they may die out. Peat is formed from rotting vegetation and the bogs in Northern Ireland have taken 10 000 years to form. The conditions needed for peat to grow are shown in Resource D.

Resource D ▼

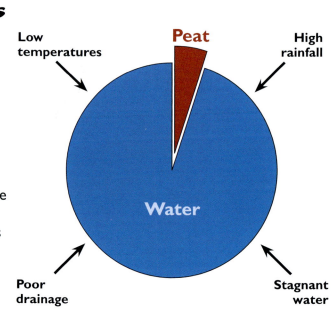

Resource E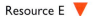

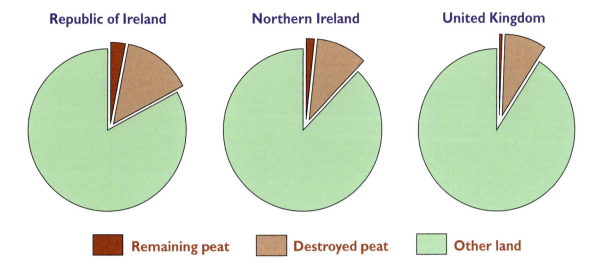

Republic of Ireland **Northern Ireland** **United Kingdom**

■ **Remaining peat**   ■ **Destroyed peat**   ■ **Other land**

Resource E shows why peat is a threatened environment.

There are two main types of peat bog found in Northern Ireland:

- **Blanket bogs:** these are carpets of peat which extend over a large area of land.
  They are found mainly in upland areas, eg the Mournes and Sperrins.
- **Raised bogs:** these are dome shaped bogs which have developed on small lakes in low lying areas, eg Peatlands Park.

Resource F shows where blanket bogs and raised bogs are found in Northern Ireland.

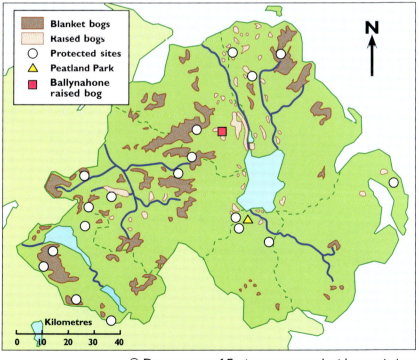

Blanket bogs
Raised bogs
○ Protected sites
△ Peatland Park
■ Ballynahone raised bog

Kilometres
0 10 20 30 40

N

© Department of Environment, used with permission

Resource F ▲

Blanket bog on the Antrim Plateau

Ballynahone raised bog

The ecosystem of peat bogs is unique as the plants and animals that live there have adapted to living in an acidic, nutrient-poor, wet environment. Plants include sphagnum moss, liverwort, sundew and heather. Animals and birds include frogs, snipe, hares, grouse and lapwings. Some of these are shown in Resource G.

Resource G ▼

Sphagnum moss

Sundew

Bog ashphodel

Bog cotton

Red grouse

Lapwing

Resource H shows why so much of our peatland has been lost. If we are not careful, we will lose the remainder of it for the same reasons.

Resource H ▶

Fuel

Horticulture/ Gardening

Reafforestation

Land reclamation for farming

Peat moss is a favourite compost for gardeners.

There are peat-free alternatives.

Many of our peat bogs are cut to provide peat for horticulture and gardening (photograph A). The peat is dried out by digging deep ditches to drain it (photograph B). Then it is sucked up by huge vacuum machines (photograph C) or cut into long sausage shapes by machines (photograph D). Once this happens the plants and animals lose their habitat and the land is not much use for anything.

Peat which has been milled is ready for transport; it will be bagged and sold in garden centres.

Peat extraction south of Lough Neagh

Ditches are cut to dry the bog out.

Cut peat on Cuilcagh Mountain

The Department of Agriculture and Rural Development (DARD) encourages farmers to use the older methods for cutting peat. This involves cutting by hand rather than by machine. The bank is cut vertically so that only a small area of vegetation is removed. Plants from the top can be moved as turves to the bottom and this encourages regeneration. The pools created at the bottom of the bank also encourage regeneration (photograph E).

In 1986 there was a danger that Ballynahone bog would be drained and that the peat would be extracted for horticulture. As with issues dealt with earlier, we will see what the problem is, what groups are involved, what decision has been taken and who are the winners and losers.

The problem

The owners of the bog submitted an application to extract peat from Ballynahone bog – one of the best remaining examples of a raised bog in Northern Ireland. It should have been designated an Area of Special Scientific Interest (ASSI) to protect it, but this had not been done.

The groups involved

The peat company
We will provide 27 jobs in an area of high unemployment and help to secure over 40 jobs elsewhere.

Local residents
We would be concerned about noise and dust pollution in the area. The roads cannot take the increased lorry traffic and if they are widened our children may be at risk.

Local farmers
Draining the bog may lead to increased flooding in the area. The area is already liable to flood.

Environmentalists
The bog is one of the few sites in Northern Ireland for the Small Heath Butterfly. It contains 20 species of plants which are rare or threatened in Northern Ireland. One of our best game fishing rivers – the Moyola – could be polluted by the peat.

The Industrial Development Board (IDB)
We need to encourage these firms to move here to provide jobs. If we make things difficult they will take their money elsewhere and this site could provide over £50 million.

School leaver
I need a job and a wage, not 20 rare plants and a butterfly!

Local haulage firm
The contract to remove the peat is worth having. There will be 4 lorries a day leaving the site for 20–25 years. We could make a lot of money and guarantee employment for 4 drivers.

On a copy of the diagram below, place the groups involved on the appropriate side of the argument. Choose one of the groups you have selected and give reasons why they have been placed there. Once you have discussed and decided on the issue, you will find the authority's decision on page 107.

Resource 1 ▶

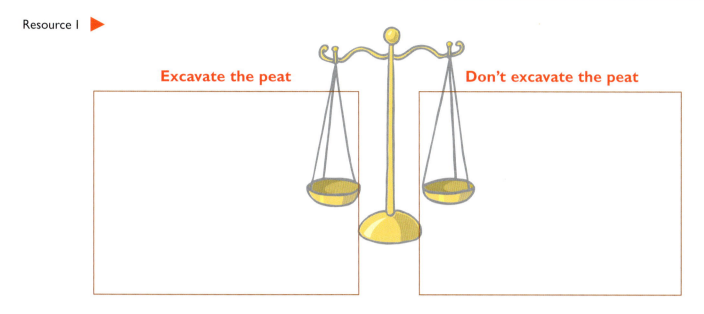

Excavate the peat   **Don't excavate the peat**

As well as extraction and draining for horticulture and gardening, peat bogs are also under threat from afforestation. Large areas of uplands in Northern Ireland have been planted with conifers such as larch, Sitka spruce, lodgepole pine and Norwegian fir. These are not native to Northern Ireland and are of limited value to wildlife. They provide another example of human activity damaging an ecosystem. The plants and animals which can exist on the bogs are squeezed out by these trees. The bog slowly dries out and the native flora and fauna can no longer exist. Their habitat has been destroyed and they cannot survive.

Conifers planted on a bog in the Antrim Plateau

Deep drainage ditches cut into a bog. This improves drainage for the young trees but dries out the bog and the plants cannot survive.

3.1 Advantage and disadvantages of ecotourism on local communities, vegetation, animals and soil

Case study   Ecosystem in the tropical grassland (savannah) of Kenya

Tropical grasslands or savannah are one of the world's ecosystems. They are found between the tropical rainforests and the desert and like all other ecosystems they contain a unique combination of plants and animals which are not found anywhere else.

Resource J shows a world map with the areas of tropical grasslands (savannah) shaded.

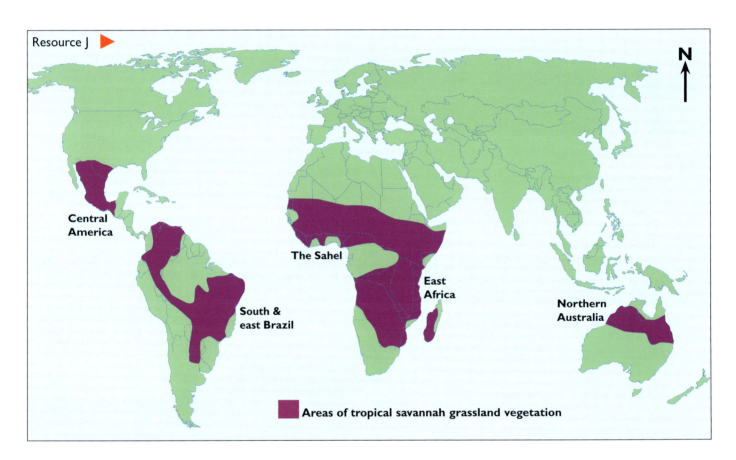

Resource J

Central America

The Sahel

South & east Brazil

East Africa

Northern Australia

N

■ Areas of tropical savannah grassland vegetation

Where is it found?

It is found between 5° and 15° north and south of the equator. Towards the equator it merges into tropical rainforest. Away from the equator it gradually changes into semi-desert and desert. Kenya is one of a number of countries of East and South Africa that contain tropical grassland (savannah).

What is the climate?

The climate can be summed up as hot all year with two wet seasons and a dry season. In Kenya these two wet spells are known as the long rains and the short rains. There are no completely dry months as tropical thunderstorms caused by convectional rain can occur at any time of year. This type of climate means that plants can grow all year round, but they have to adapt to the dry season. The rainfall poses problems for the plants and animals as it varies so much. There is a big variation from year to year in how long it lasts and how much rain falls. In some years there is a lot of rain. In other years there may be less rain. This means that the dry season also varies.

Like the plants and animals, any people who farm here have to cope with the seasons. Plants have to be sown at the start of the long rains and harvested at the end. The problem is that the farmers do not know how long the rainy season will last and they do not know how much rain will fall.

The climate for Makindu (see Resource M on page 84) is shown on the following climate table.

	Jan	Feb	Mar	Apr	May	Jun	Jul	Aug	Sept	Oct	Nov	Dec
Temp (°C)	23	24	24	24	22	21	20	21	22	23	23	23
PPT (mm)	39	28	67	107	29	2	1	1	2	29	174	108

Annual range of temperature = 4°C (Aldergrove would be 11°C)

Total PPT = 587 mm (Aldergrove is 852 mm)

How do the plants adapt to the climate?

The savannah plants adapt to the wet and dry season in the following ways:

- Grass withers down in the dry season.
- Roots remain in the ground.
- When the rains arrive the plants quickly germinate and grow.
- Some grasses grow up to four metres tall (elephant grass).
- Grasses mix in with herbs and flowers which have bulbs or tubers. These are drought resistant as well. See photograph A.
- The seeds of the plants are hard and lie dormant until the rains come.
- Trees have thorns to help protect them from hungry animals.
- Trees have deep roots to tap underground water supplies.
- Trees have tough bark to resist the heat of the dry season.
- Trees are deciduous – they lose their leaves in the dry season.
- Acacia (photograph C) and baobab (photograph B) are typical trees.

A

B

C

What animals can live here?

The grass and trees sustain a wide variety of animals which are shown in Resource K.

Consumers are grazing animals or herbivores such as antelope, wildebeest, elephant, buffalo, giraffe, rhino, bushbuck, gnu, zebra, baboons and gazelles.

In turn these animals attract a range of **predators** or **carnivores** which feed on the grazing animals. These include lions, cheetahs and leopards.

The ecosystem also includes **scavengers** who wait for the predators to finish with a carcass and then move in to feed. These include vultures, hyenas, foxes and jackals. Some of these smaller carnivores will also hunt for themselves.

Like all ecosystems the waste material and carcasses are recycled back into the ground to provide nutrients for the growing plants. **Decomposers** include dung beetles, ants and termites.

The ecosystem is even more complex than the diagram shows as it also includes large numbers of birds, insects, butterflies, lizards, rodents, snakes and smaller carnivores. These are all part of the ecosystem and form different food chains.

Savannah grassland food chain

Resource K ▶

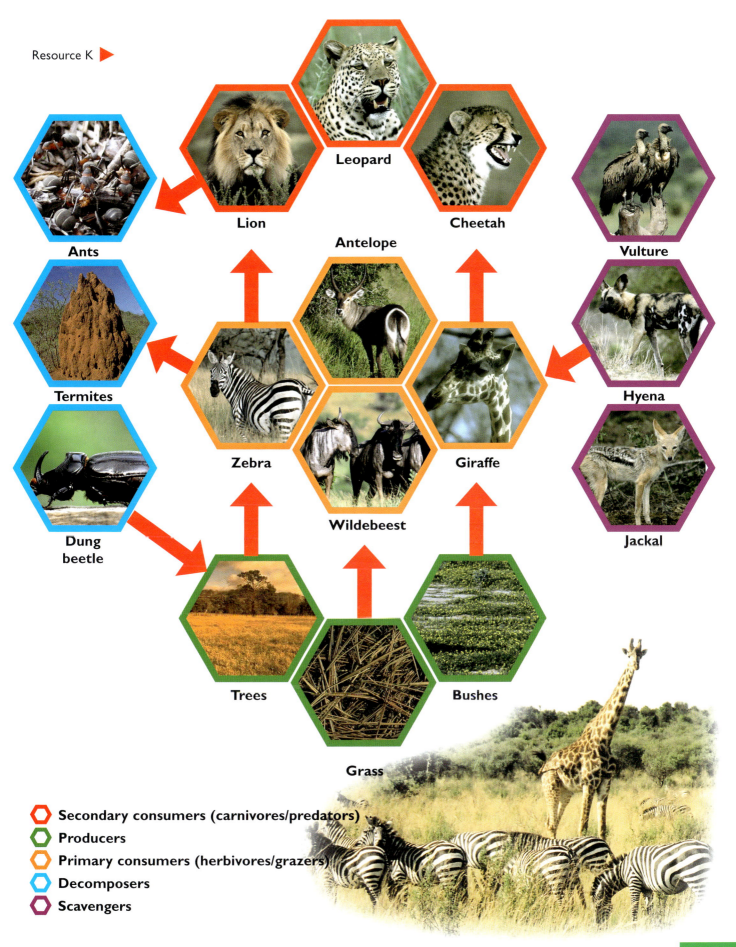

- ⬡ **Secondary consumers (carnivores/predators)**
- ⬡ **Producers**
- ⬡ **Primary consumers (herbivores/grazers)**
- ⬡ **Decomposers**
- ⬡ **Scavengers**

The number and variety of animals attract a lot of tourists. Kenya has set aside large reserves where the animals can be seen in their natural surroundings. Outside these reserves the animals are not safe as the land is needed to grow crops and the animals compete with man for food and space. Since Kenya began to develop tourism in the early 1960s there has been a big increase in tourism and it is now a major part of their economy.

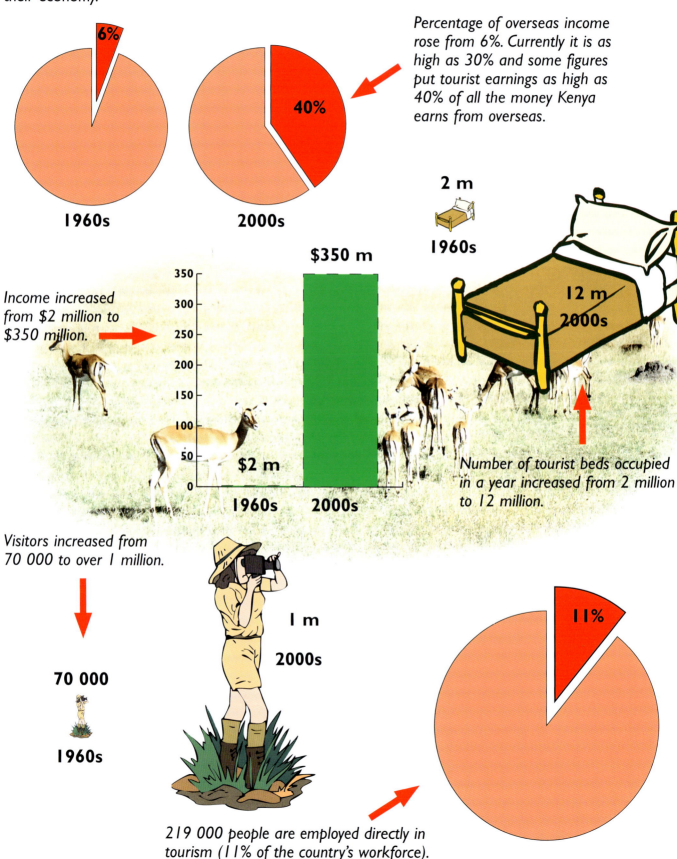

6%

1960s

40%

2000s

Percentage of overseas income rose from 6%. Currently it is as high as 30% and some figures put tourist earnings as high as 40% of all the money Kenya earns from overseas.

2 m

1960s

12 m

2000s

Income increased from $2 million to $350 million.

$350 m

$2 m

1960s   2000s

Number of tourist beds occupied in a year increased from 2 million to 12 million.

Visitors increased from 70 000 to over 1 million.

70 000

1960s

1 m

2000s

11%

219 000 people are employed directly in tourism (11% of the country's workforce).

Kenya has to look at the advantages and disadvantages of tourism.

Resource L

Advantages of tourism

- Tourists bring money into the local economy.
- Tourists provide jobs for local people as drivers, guides and rangers.
- Accommodation is needed for the tourists; this provides jobs in the hotel industry.
- Tourists need services such as electricity, water and sewage. Local people can benefit from this as well.
- Good transport links are needed and these can benefit local people or help provide jobs for them.
- Farmers can grow crops that can be sold to the hotels and guesthouses.
- Local craftsmen can find a market for their products.

Disadvantages of tourism

- Local people may not have access to the services provided for the tourists.
- 'Rich' tourists provide easy targets for thieves.
- Western values and attitudes affect the local culture and community.
- Young people are not content to stay in the area and want to move away for a better lifestyle. Contact with tourists unsettles them.
- Much of the money spent by tourists goes out of the country, or to the government. As little as 15% may reach the local economy.

The game parks have been in existence for over 40 years. In this time, problems have arisen as a result of the numbers of visitors:

- Local people were driven off their land so that the reserves could be created.
- Too many tourists mean that the local ecosystem is put under pressure and the wildlife can suffer. Tourists are in danger of destroying the wildlife areas they have come to see.
- The tyre tracks of four-wheel drive vehicles cause soil erosion (see photograph A).
- Animals are disturbed as drivers come too close so that the tourists get good pictures. The better the pictures the bigger the tip at the end of the day.
- Balloon safaris can unsettle grazing animals and stampede them across the plains. The gas burners are noisy and shadows upset the grazing herds.
- In drier years in popular game reserves, some areas have been reduced to dust bowls – vehicles have removed all the vegetation as they crisscrossed the savannah trying to get close to the animals.

A

In the 1990s some tour operators tried to introduce ecotourism. This is defined as "Responsible travel to natural areas that conserves the environment and sustains the well-being of local people." There are seven aspects to ecotourism. It:

- Respects local culture
- Involves travel to natural areas
- Minimises impact
- Builds environmental awareness
- Provides direct financial benefits for conservation
- Provides financial benefits and empowerment for local people
- Supports human rights and democratic movements

This breaks down into three components:

- It is essentially 'nature-based'.
- It implies a commitment to the conservation of nature.
- It means that the local community should derive benefits from tourism and should be able to take part.

Ecotourism is growing at between 10% and 15% per year. If the local people see that they can benefit from tourism then they will play their part by looking after the ecosystem and the wildlife which attracts the tourists.

Resource M ▼

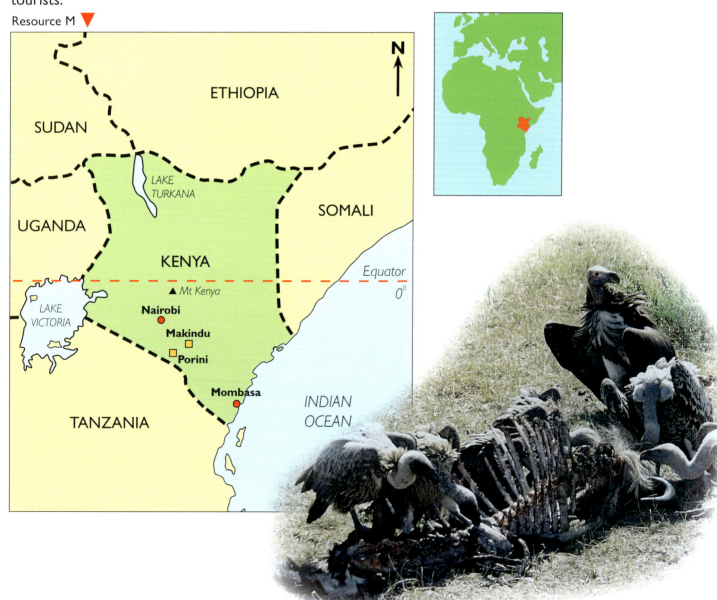

Case study   Ecotourism in Kenya

Porini ecotourism

Porini is Kiswahili for 'in the wilds'.
This camp is just north of Amboseli in an area known as Eselenkei (pronounced 'Selengay'). Resource M shows the location.

In May 1997 Porini agreed with the local Masai community to set aside an area of 75 000 hectares as a reserve for wildlife. Cattle had overgrazed this area and much of the wildlife had been hunted for meat. The Masai received the following benefits from the deal:

- Rent for the lease of the area, increasing by 10% each year
- An entry fee for each visitor, increasing by 10% each year
- Local labour employed to construct 70-kilometre roads and viewing tracks
- A warden and 14 game scouts employed to carry out patrols and protect wildlife
- Sixteen people employed in the camp (photograph C)
- Two boreholes for water have been drilled in local villages.
- Money has been given to the local primary school and students have been helped to go on to further education.

In return for these benefits the Masai agreed not to graze their cattle in the reserve and not to hunt in it. Porini was then able to develop an ecotourist facility with the following features:

- A maximum of 12 tourists in camp at one time
- Accommodation in large tents, not permanent buildings (photograph D)
- No generators – power is provided by a solar power system (photograph B)
- All rubbish is taken to Nairobi for recycling or composted on site.
- Water heating and cooking does not use bush charcoal which contributes to deforestation. Instead they use environmentally-friendly briquettes.
- Water and sewage is directed into septic tanks which do not pollute the water table.

Since the operation started there has been an increase in the wildlife seen on the reserve. Elephants have returned for the first time in 20 years and lions, cheetahs, giraffe, zebra, wildebeest, impala and gazelles are common. The local people are committed to conserving the wildlife because they can see and share in the benefits.

Questions

1 Study the first photograph, which shows an area of blanket bog in Cuilcagh Mountain Park.
Sheep have been excluded from one part of the area photographed. Answer the following questions. The
number of marks for each question are given. Questions with one mark have a one word answer. In
questions with two or three marks you would be expected to write two or three lines.

(a) From which part of the area photographed have sheep been excluded – X or Y?   (1)

(b) Give a reason for your answer to (a).   (3)

(c) State and explain one reason why farmers would be tempted to overgraze an area of blanket bog such as
that shown in the photograph.   (3)

(d) State and explain one reason why farmers might allow commercial peat-cutting on land such as this.
                                                                                        (3)

2 Study the second photograph which shows an area of blanket bog on Cuilcagh Mountain that has been cut
over for peat.

(a) State one use for the peat which has been extracted from the area.   (1)

(b) State and explain two reasons why an environmentalist might object to this activity. (6)

(c) The Department of Agriculture and Rural Development (DARD) made this area an
Environmentally Sensitive Area (ESA) in 1993. State and explain one consequence
this would have for the farmer.   (3)

3 Look at photographs A and B which show two views of
the Porini ecotourism camp at Eselenkei in Kenya, then
answer the questions which follow.

(a) What is meant by ecotourism?   (2)

(b) The camp uses tents instead of permanent buildings. Explain how this is a more sustainable type of
tourism.   (2)

(c) The camp limits the number of tourists to 12 at any one time. Explain how this helps to limit damage to
the environment.   (3)

(d) State and explain why tourists like those in the photograph would be willing to pay extra money to stay
in an ecotourist camp.   (3)

(e) State and explain why the local Masai tribesmen are less likely to hunt and kill wildlife as a result of the
camp being established.   (3)

(f) Tourists who visit the camp have to pay a fee to the Masai community. State and explain two ways the
money could be used to help the local Masai villages.   (6)

THEME D

Population and Resources

This theme concentrates on the salient features of population distribution, structure and growth. The growth of population, combined with developments in technology, has put increased pressure on natural resources. This creates complex problems which cannot be readily solved.

1.1 Physical and economic factors affecting distribution and density

Resource A shows a population density map of Northern Ireland divided by council areas. The population distribution depends on physical and human/economic factors:

Physical factors

Climate

Relief

Soil

Position

Water supply

Human/economic factors

Transport

Economic Activity

Resources

Infrastructure

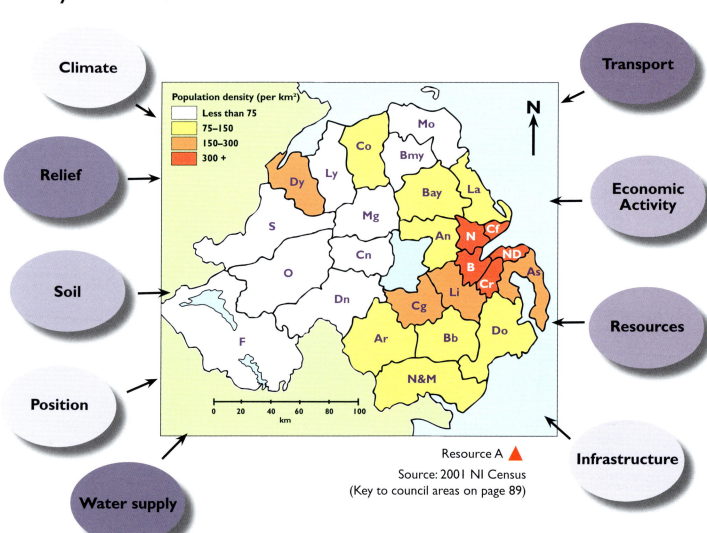

Population density (per km²)
- Less than 75
- 75–150
- 150–300
- 300 +

N

0 20 40 60 80 100 km

Resource A ▲

Source: 2001 NI Census
(Key to council areas on page 89)

The reasons for population distribution in Northern Ireland are as follows:

- It is part of the UK so people tend to live on the east coast where there are easy transport links to the UK.
- The west of the province is hillier.
- The climate is drier towards the east.
- The soils in the west are less fertile and harder to work with.
- Jobs are easier to find in the Belfast Metropolitan Urban Area. (This is made up of the council areas of Belfast, Castlereagh, North Down, Lisburn, Newtownabbey and Carrickfergus.)
- There is another densely populated area in the north-west in the Derry Urban Area.

Resource B ▶

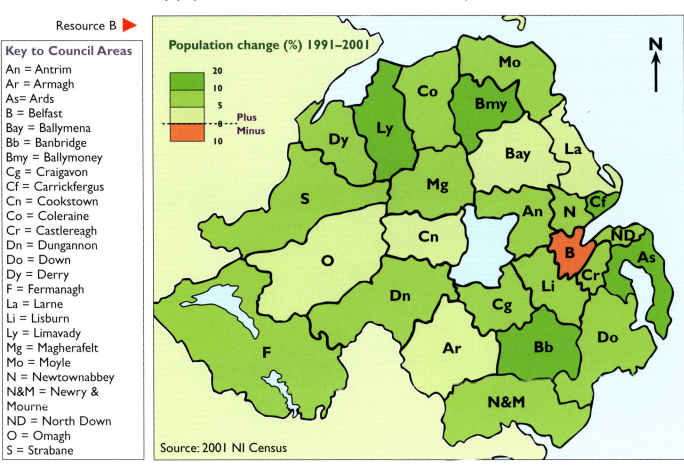

Key to Council Areas

An = Antrim
Ar = Armagh
As= Ards
B = Belfast
Bay = Ballymena
Bb = Banbridge
Bmy = Ballymoney
Cg = Craigavon
Cf = Carrickfergus
Cn = Cookstown
Co = Coleraine
Cr = Castlereagh
Dn = Dungannon
Do = Down
Dy = Derry
F = Fermanagh
La = Larne
Li = Lisburn
Ly = Limavady
Mg = Magherafelt
Mo = Moyle
N = Newtownabbey
N&M = Newry & Mourne
ND = North Down
O = Omagh
S = Strabane

Source: 2001 NI Census

Resource B shows the percentage changes that have taken place in Northern Ireland between the 1991 and the 2001 censuses. This change is made up of three parts:

- Birth rate – the number of babies born per 1000 of the population
- Death rate – the number of deaths per 1000 of the population
- Migration – the difference between the numbers of people who move in (immigrants) and move out (emigrants)

All of these can be positive or negative and can lead to an increase or a decrease in the population. Northern Ireland's population has increased from 1 607 295 in 1991 to 1 689 319 in 2001 – an increase of 82 024 or 5.1%. The following points can be noted:

- Every council area except Belfast has registered an increase.
- Belfast's decrease is due to counterurbanisation (see page 124).
- The areas in the Belfast Metropolitan Urban Area have all shown an increase (see pages 125–6).
- Areas in the west of the province generally show lower increases.

Case study Italy

The UK and Italy are very similar in population, although Italy has a bigger area. In this case study we will look at the population distribution and density patterns in Italy and then try to explain why these happen.

Country	Population	Area (km²)	Density (per km²)
UK	60 million	244 820	245
Italy	58 million	301 230	193

Resource C ▶

Resource C shows the regions of Italy.

What is Italy's population distribution and density?

Resource D shows a table of Italy's regions with their population and population density (per square kilometre).

Resource D ▼

	Region	Population (millions)	Population density
1	Piedmont	4.2	166
2	Aosta Valley	1.2	37
3	Lombardy	9	290
4	Trentino Alto Adige	0.9	69
5	Veneto	4.5	379
6	Friuli-Venezia Giulia	1.2	246
7	Liguria	1.6	151
8	Emilia-Romagna	4	180
9	Tuscany	3.5	152
10	Umbria	0.8	98
11	Marches	1.5	152
12	Lazio	5.1	297
13	Abruzzo	1.3	117
14	Molise	0.3	72
15	Campania	5.7	420
16	Apulia	4	208
17	Basilicata	0.6	60
18	Calabria	2	133
19	Sicily	5	193
20	Sardinia	1.6	68

On a very simple level we can see that 30.1 million people live in the northern regions (1–9), 9 million live in the central area (10–14) and 18.9 million live in the south or Mezzogiorno (15–20).

Campania (Region 15). High mountains close to the sea make settlement difficult. There is a shortage of flat land.

A better way is to look at a colour coded or choropleth map — see Resource E.

Resource E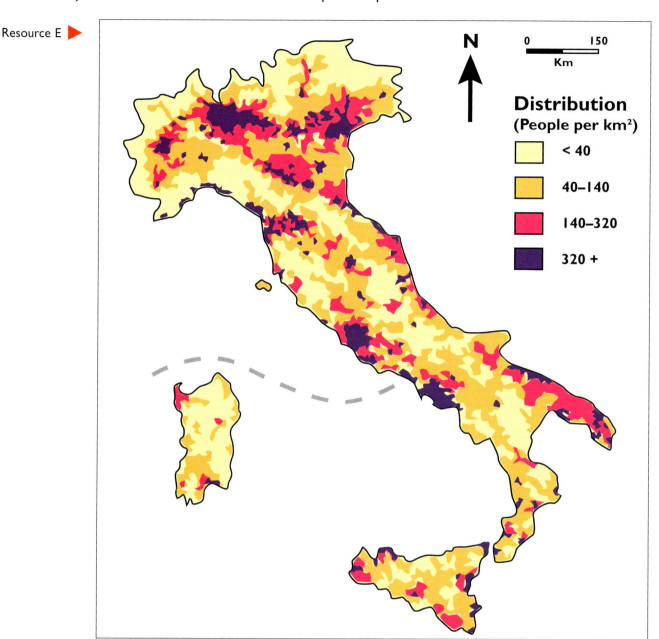

Distribution
(People per km²)

	< 40
	40–140
	140–320
	320 +

This shows us that there are some areas of Italy which are densely populated while others are sparsely populated. The choropleth map also shows us that the north is more densely populated than the south. There are also two densely populated areas along the west coast and one in the south-east in Apulia.

Tuscany (Region 9). Steep hills suffering from soil erosion mean that the area will be sparsely populated. ▶

Resource F shows us a map of population density. Population density is given in people per square kilometre. This allows us to compare the area and population of regions. Population density is found using the following formula:

$$D = \frac{P}{A} \quad \text{where } D = \text{Density}$$
$$P = \text{Population}$$
$$A = \text{Area}$$

This map confirms the high density in the north of Italy in Lombardy and Veneto. It also shows the two densely populated areas on the west coast – Lazio and Campania – plus Apulia in the south-east.

Resource F ▶

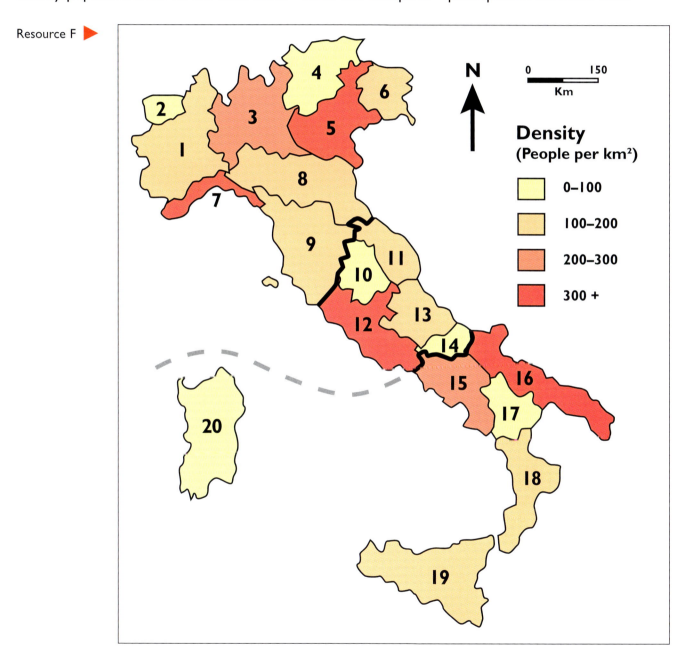

Density
(People per km²)

☐ 0–100
☐ 100–200
☐ 200–300
☐ 300 +

Population distribution is not static – it is always changing and moving. People migrate from one area to another for a variety of reasons. Resource G shows the changes there have been since the previous census in 1991.

Resource G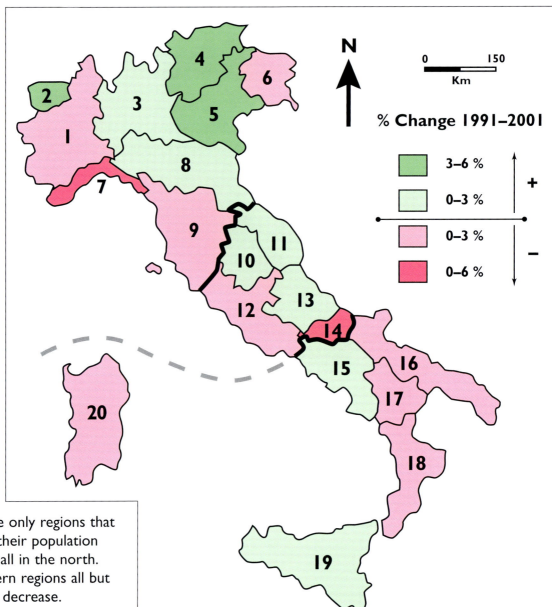

N

0   150
Km

% Change 1991–2001

	3–6 %	+
	0–3 %	
	0–3 %	
	0–6 %	–

On this map the only regions that have increased their population by over 3% are all in the north. Of the 7 southern regions all but 2 have shown a decrease. When we put all this evidence together we see that the north of Italy is more densely populated than the south and is increasing in population. The south of Italy has less people, is more sparsely populated and the population is decreasing.

Florence is one of Italy's large cities. These attract people and are densely populated. ▶

The population distribution depends on physical and human/economic factors:

Physical factors

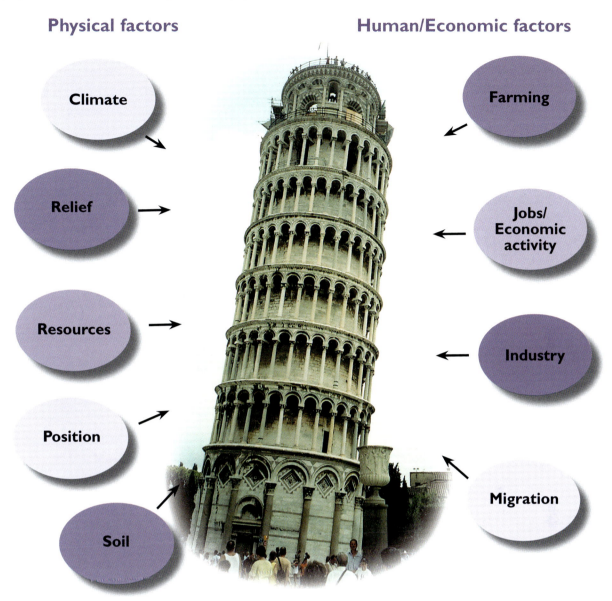

Climate

Relief

Resources

Position

Soil

Human/Economic factors

Farming

Jobs/
Economic
activity

Industry

Migration

How can we explain the differences in Italy's population distribution and density?

1. Position

Look at Resource H. This shows Italy's position in Europe. You can see that the northern regions of Italy are much closer to the main area of Europe while the southern regions of Italy are closer to north Africa. People living in Calabria or Sicily have a long way to travel to reach France and Germany – up to 1000 kilometres. This makes it difficult to export food, crops or manufactured goods. Farms and factories in the north have easier access to markets.

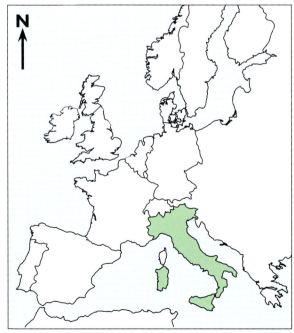

Resource H ▶

95

2. Relief

Study Resource I. This shows a relief map of Italy. The Alps form the northern border with Europe. They are over 4000 metres high, the land is steep and farming is limited, so these areas are sparsely populated.

A chain of mountains called the Apennines runs down the centre of Italy. They are not as high as the Alps but they are steep and are sparsely populated.

The only large area of flat fertile land is the valley of the River Po in the north.

Further south the flat areas are small and hemmed in by the Apennines and the sea. People are attracted to the flatter land in the north.

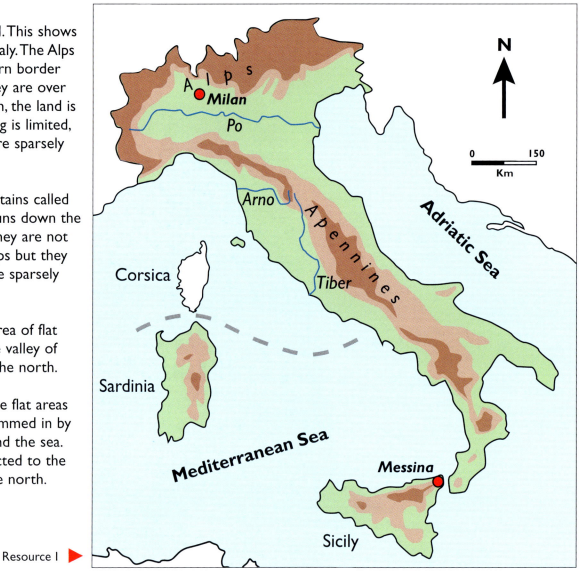

Resource I ▶

3. Soil

The soils in the north of Italy are more fertile. The best soils are found in the Po valley where the River Po has flooded over the land and left a rich fertile soil called alluvium. The south of Italy has thinner, less fertile soils which have been eroded in many places by the heavy winter rains. Overgrazing and deforestation have contributed to this problem. The only good soils in the south are small flat areas near the coast at the base of the hills. This makes it easier for farmers in the north to make a living.

4. Climate

Italy stretches over 1000 kilometres from north to south so there is quite a difference in climate. The climate in the North is more European while the climate in the south is more African. Look at the climate statistics for Milan and Messina. Milan is in the Lombardy Plain while Messina is in Sicily.

Milan – 107 m

	Jan	Feb	Mar	Apr	May	Jun	Jul	Aug	Sept	Oct	Nov	Dec
Temp (°C)	1	4	8	13	17	21	24	23	19	13	7	3
PPT (mm)	61	58	72	85	99	81	68	80	82	116	106	75

Annual range of temperature = 23°C
Total PPT = 983 mm

Messina – 193 m

	Jan	Feb	Mar	Apr	May	Jun	Jul	Aug	Sept	Oct	Nov	Dec
Temp (°C)	12	12	13	15	19	23	26	26	24	20	16	14
PPT (mm)	114	113	85	60	33	15	17	26	56	104	103	120

Annual range of temperature = 14°C
Total PPT = 846 mm

The climate in the north is more temperate; it has a smaller temperature range, heavier rainfall and no dry season. Climate in the south is more typically Mediterranean with heavy winter rain, higher summer temperatures and a definite drought in summer. The heavy winter rain has led to soil erosion on the steep slopes of the Apennines.

5. Resources
The South of Italy has very few resources to provide the raw materials for industry. The only important mines are for gold and bauxite in Sardinia. In the north there is hydro electric power (HEP) from the Alps, gypsum, lime, marble, lignite, and geothermal energy. Petroleum and marble are found in both areas.

6. Farming
The flatter land and better climate in the north means that farmers can grow a better variety of crops which they can sell in Italy or export north to the rest of Europe. Irrigation is essential for farmers in the south if they are to diversify away from the traditional crops of wheat, grapes and olives. Farms in the north are larger, more commercial and have up-to-date technology. Farms in the south are smaller, family-run and lack technology. Many of them are at or near subsistence level. The relief and climate of the area means that sheep and goats have been widely kept. They overgrazed areas already suffering from soil erosion leading to large parts of the Apennines being reduced to bare rock where nothing could be grown at all.

7. Industry
The north has always been the centre of industry. Industries have been based in the 'Golden Triangle' of Milan, Turin and Genoa and in the port of Venice. Industries included cars, engineering, fashion/textiles, glass, white goods and shipbuilding. As industries grew and developed they attracted other industries to the area and the multiplier effect took over.

8. Jobs/Economic activity
With the growth of cities and industries and rapid urbanisation in the late nineteenth century, more jobs were created in secondary and tertiary industries. This attracted more people which resulted in more jobs. Milan also became the centre of banking and finance in Italy which attracted jobs to the area.

9. Migration
A combination of all the above factors meant that the south of Italy was and is an area of out-migration. This migration occurred in three stages – firstly to urban areas in the south, then to urban areas in the north or the Americas, and finally to other areas in Europe. In the 1960s and 1970s it is estimated that 2.5 million people from the south moved to the north. Many of these people were unskilled and in the 21–35 age group. In the last 40 years 63% of Italians migrating overseas have come from the south of Italy. The three main reasons for leaving were unemployment, scarcity of land and poverty.

2.3 Population structure/pyramids

Case study   Population structure of Portstewart and Magherafelt

Magherafelt *(Population 8300)*

Portstewart *(Population 7800)*

Population structure depends on three things:

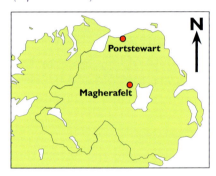

- **Birth rates**
  The number of births per thousand per year
- **Death rates**
  The number of deaths per thousand per year
- **Migration**
  The number of people who have moved into or out of the area

Using census data from the ten-year census it is possible to look at the structure of a town, council area or a country. Resource J shows the population pyramids for Portstewart and Magherafelt based on the 1991 census returns.

Resource J ▼

Source: 1991 NI Census

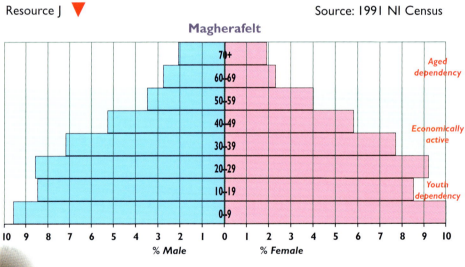

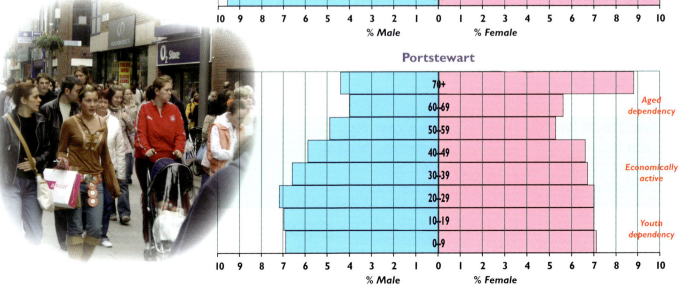

Governments have a rough idea of changes by checking birth and death certificates every year, as people are legally obliged to register these. They cannot keep up with in-migration or out-migration as there is no legal requirement for people to keep councils informed of their movements. The census data collected in 2001 gave the planners a chance to see what has happened since 1991, and to adjust their plans if they thought they needed more or fewer places in schools, hospitals and residential homes.

Resource K ▼

Source: 2001 NI Census

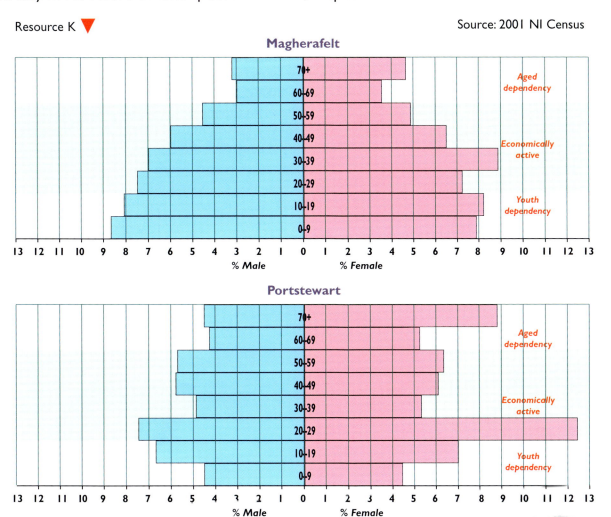

By comparing the population pyramids of Portstewart and Magherafelt in 1991 (Resource J) and 2001 (Resource K) the following trends can be noticed:

- The birth rate in Magherafelt is increasing.
- The birth rate in Portstewart is decreasing.
- Over 32% of Magherafelt's population is under 20.
- Only 22% of Portstewart's population is under 20.
- Over 14% of Magherafelt's population is over 60.
- Over 22% of Portstewart's population is over 60.
- There has been a big influx of 20–29 year old females into Portstewart.

Portstewart may need more services and money for its elderly population. A higher percentage of older people puts a greater strain on doctors, health clinics and social services support. Magherafelt will need to ensure that there are enough nursery and primary places for the 0–9 age group. They may also need to increase the childcare facilities for the town. Remember that these graphs are dynamic and every ten years the bars move up. The planners have to look ahead and predict what services will be needed in the future.

3.2 Sustainable approaches to energy use and development of renewable energy resources

Case study   Energy resources in Northern Ireland

Increasing population means an increasing demand for energy. The population of Northern Ireland has increased by just under 400 000 since 1900. In 1900 very few people had electricity; now there are 1.68 million people who all need electricity for lighting and heating. They also need power to heat and light shops, offices and factories. Most people are not satisfied with basic technology – they want the latest labour-saving devices and in many cases they want more than one of them. In 1950 a few houses had one television. Now virtually every house has one television and many houses have more than one. They also have DVD players, fridges, freezers, dishwashers, cookers, radios, music centres and a host of other electrical appliances. This increased demand for electricity means that the country does not have the resources to generate enough. It has to import the energy resources it needs. Resource L shows Northern Ireland's energy requirements compared to the UK and Republic of Ireland. As you can see, most of these come from non-renewable resources which will eventually run out and are not sustainable in the long run.

Resource L ▶

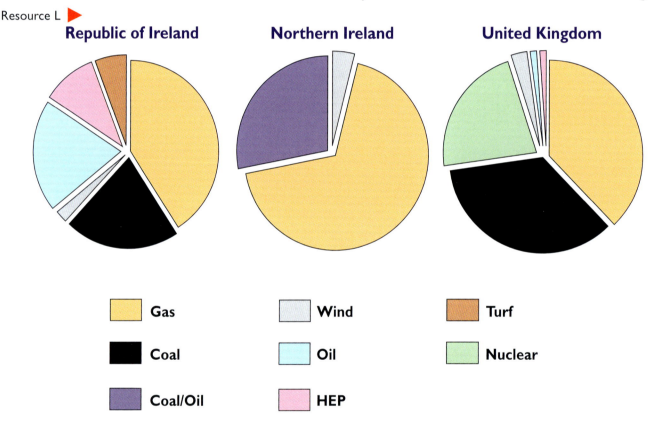

Republic of Ireland   **Northern Ireland**   **United Kingdom**

	Gas		Wind		Turf
	Coal		Oil		Nuclear
	Coal/Oil		HEP		

Like many other MEDCs, Northern Ireland needs to find a more sustainable approach to its energy requirements. A sustainable approach to the use of energy is crucial to people and the environment.

At present Northern Ireland's energy requirements are met by three large power stations shown on Resource M. This can be supplemented by importing power from Scotland through an undersea cable. The power stations all run on imported fossil fuels. When they are burnt they produce waste gases which contribute to acid rain and global warming. Northern Ireland is committed to generating 10% of its needs from renewable resources by 2010. A switch to renewable resources would lead to the following benefits:

- Less dependency on imported fuels
- Less production of pollution which leads to acid rain and global warming
- Less money going overseas to pay for imported fuel
- Less risk of being held hostage to higher prices by overseas suppliers

Resource M ▶

Electricity generation in Northern Ireland

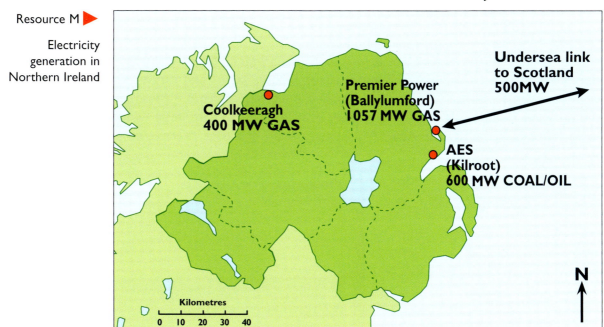

Coolkeeragh 400 MW GAS

Premier Power (Ballylumford) 1057 MW GAS

Undersea link to Scotland 500MW

AES (Kilroot) 600 MW COAL/OIL

N

Kilometres
0 10 20 30 40

Northern Ireland needs to replace fossil fuels with renewable resources, so that we have a more sustainable use of energy.

There are seven main sources of renewable energy. All of these resources are sustainable, and do not pollute the environment. However, many of them are expensive to build, are not suited to Northern Ireland, and at present cannot compete on price with electricity generated from fossil fuels. Starting with the least likely to be used in Northern Ireland, they are as follows:

- Geothermal power
- Wave power
- Tidal Power
- Solar power
- Biomass/biogas power
- Hydro electric power (HEP)
- Wind power

We will look at each of these in turn and see what the potential is for each one in Northern Ireland.

Geothermal power

This is generated from hot rocks or hot water under the Earth's surface. A test borehole at Larne showed that there was no potential for geothermal power in Northern Ireland. The rocks are simply not hot enough.

Wave power

This has potential on coasts which face west towards the Atlantic Ocean. The coasts of Northern Ireland face either north or east, so there is no potential for wave power in Northern Ireland.

Tidal power

This uses the rise and fall of the tide to generate electricity. Strangford Lough and Carlingford Lough provide the best opportunities in Northern Ireland but the tidal range is too low. Strangford Lough has a range of 3.3 metres compared to the only tidal power station in Europe on the River Rance in France, which has a range of over 11 metres. The cost of building the barrage is too high and there are strong environmental concerns at both sites. A feasibility study has been started to look at tidal power. This is like a wind turbine underneath which is turned by water. Even if this proves possible it will be some time before we get power from it.

Solar power

This uses direct sunlight to generate power or to heat water. Photovoltaics can be used in remote locations for road signs and weather stations (see below). Yachts and caravans can also use photovoltaic power. Some houses and offices have solar panels built into the roof – these give a supply of hot water which saves on electricity costs. Other houses are designed to have large windows facing south – these soak up free heat from the sun. Apart from these small-scale uses, there is no potential for solar power in Northern Ireland.

Weather station and road sign using solar power

Biomass/biogas power

This can use a variety of resources such as willow, solid household waste, farm slurry, sewage sludge, straw and landfill gas. They are either burnt directly and used like fossil fuels, or they are used to produce methane which is used like natural gas to heat water. In Northern Ireland there have been a number of proposals for using sewage sludge, animal waste and solid municipal waste which have not yet started. There are two schemes using willow. This is the most likely way forward as willow is easy to grow and farmers may be able to switch to willow as other types of farming come under pressure.

Willow trees being grown

Willow chips ready for burning

Hydro electric power (HEP)

This uses the power of falling water. Scotland has several large schemes which generate 1230 MW. Small schemes generate 70 MW in Scotland, 23 MW in England and Wales, but only 3.4 MW in Northern Ireland. Environmental considerations make it unlikely that Northern Ireland will ever have a large-scale scheme. There are 9 small-scale schemes, the largest of which is at Sion Mills, County Tyrone. There is potential for more small-scale schemes which can sell electricity to the national grid.

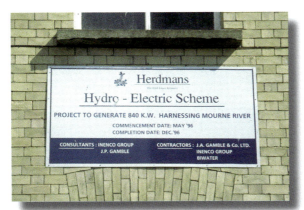

Northern Ireland's largest HEP scheme

HEP turbine

Wind power

Of all the renewable resources this is the one which has the most potential. Power is generated by wind turbines grouped together in wind farms. Each turbine is around 40 metres high and wind farms usually have 10 or more turbines. Northern Ireland has 12 wind farms in operation with proposals for 11 more. They are shown in Resource N overleaf.

One wind farm produces enough power for 4000–5000 homes. We can build more wind farms but we will always need other power sources for the following reasons:

- Replacing Ballylumford Premier Power station would need nearly 2000 turbines. Where would we put them all?
- Power is generated only when the wind is blowing at between 5 and 25 metres per second. That is Force 4 to 9 on the Beaufort Scale. Turbines work best when the wind is Force 7 to 9. This only happens on average for 3 minutes in every hour!
- Turbines have to be in exposed windy regions. These are usually the mountain areas which are often Areas of Outstanding Natural Beauty (AONBs). Too many turbines would lead to visual pollution.

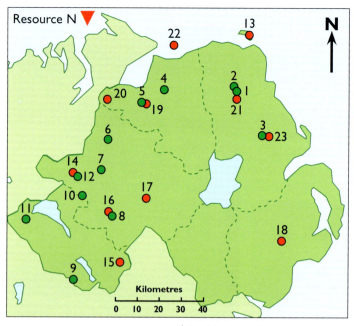

Resource N ▼

Number	Location	Turbines
1	Corkey, Cloghmills	10
2	Slievenahanaghan	1
3	Elliot's Hill, Tildarg	10
4	Rigged Hill, Limavady	10
5	Altahullion, Limavady	20
6	Owenreagh	10
7	Bessy Bell, Newtownstewart	10
8	Lendrum's Bridge, Fintona	20
9	Slieve Rushen, Derrylin	10
10	Tappaghan Mtn, Lack	13
11	Callagheen, Belleek	13
12	Lough Hill, Drumquin	7
13	Rathlin Island	3*
14	Bin Mtn, Castlederg	7
15	Garrane, Rosslea	10
16	Hunter's Hill, Fintona	7–10
17	Slieve Divena	up to 12
18	Slieve Croob	3
19	Altahullion extension	9
20	Curryfree, New Buildings	8
21	Gruig, Corkey, Cloghmills	14
22	Tunes Plateau offshore, Portstewart	50–85
23	Wolf Bog, Tildarg	5

● Existing wind farms

● Proposed wind farms

* Rathlin is no longer operational but there are plans to replace the three turbines.

Wind power now supplies between 3% and 4% of our energy needs, and is generating around 100 MW.

SUMMARY:
Northern Ireland needs to generate 10% of its energy requirements from renewable resources by 2010. This target will be difficult to achieve.

Case study   Portstewart Wind Farm

Wind farms can be controversial; they have their supporters and opponents. The most controversial scheme is the proposed £200 million wind farm on Tunes Plateau. It will put between 50 and 85 turbines 5–10 kilometres off Portstewart in the Foyle Estuary. The arguments can be summed up as follows:

Resource O ▶

Supporters of the scheme say

- Wind energy is renewable.
- No greenhouse gases will be produced.
- The scheme will provide electricity for 170 000 houses – 28% of Northern Ireland's total.
- This scheme will provide 7–9% of our energy needs so we will meet our 10% target for renewable energy in 2010.
- 80% of tourists surveyed said that the turbines would either have no effect on their decision to visit the area or would encourage them to return.

Opponents of the scheme say

- There will be a danger to migrating birds.
- The seabed will be destroyed.
- Inshore fishing will be affected and jobs may be lost.
- This is an Area of Outstanding Natural Beauty; the turbines will ruin the view from the Causeway Coast.
- Tourists will be driven away from the area and tourism is the biggest source of income.

The argument is ongoing at the time of going to press and it may go to a public enquiry. Check the news headlines. When a decision is made it is likely that the loser will appeal and the arguments will run and run.

Questions

1 Study Resource P which shows population pyramids for Northern Ireland in 1991 and 2001 and answer the questions which follow.

Resource P ▶

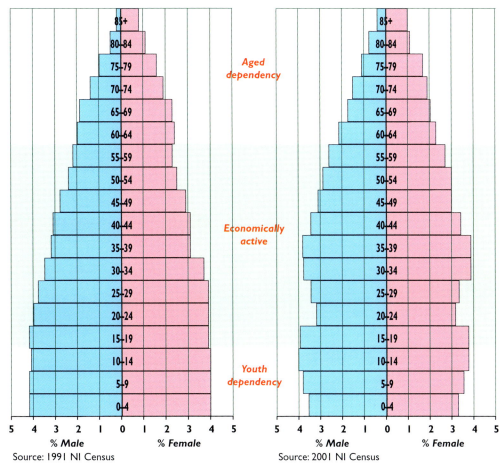

Source: 1991 NI Census   Source: 2001 NI Census

(a) State whether the following statements are true or false.   (4)

   In 1991 there were more females than males in the 85+ age group.
   In 2001 there were more females than males in the 0–4 age group.
   In 2001 the youth dependency population was over 30%.
   In 1991 there were more aged dependency females than there were males.

(b) These population pyramids are typical of an MEDC. Using evidence from Resource P state and explain two reasons why you think this is an MEDC.   (6)

(c) "The birth rate in Northern Ireland is falling." Using evidence from Resource P to support your answer say whether you agree or disagree with this statement.   (3)

2 Study Resource Q which shows the population of Northern Ireland by age groups, then answer the questions which follow.

Resource Q

(a) What is the youth dependency population for 1991?   (1)

(b) What is the difference between the aged dependency figures for 1991 and 2001?   (2)

	1991 (%)	2001 (%)
Youth dependency	24	22
Economically active	59	60
Aged dependency	17	18

(c) The ratio between all dependents and economically active in 2001 is:

      50–50   40–60   30–70   20–80

    Choose the correct answer from the four options.   (1)

(d) The government expects the percentage of aged dependency to rise in the future. State and explain two consequences for Northern Ireland as a result of an increasing number of people over 60.   (6)

3 Study Resource R, which shows an aerial photograph of Coolkeeragh Power Station, County Londonderry, and answer the questions which follow.

Resource R ▼

Esler Crawford Photography

(a) Match up the following features with the correct letter from the photograph.

    Oil storage   …

    Lough Foyle   …

    Jetty   …

    Car park   …

    Farmland   …   (5)

(b) Give two reasons why all power stations in Northern Ireland, including this one at Coolkeeragh, are built on the coast.   (4)

(c) Coolkeeragh uses oil to generate electricity. State and explain one reason why this is not a sustainable use of resources.   (2)

(d) State and explain why the people living at 3 in the photograph might object to the site of the power station.   (2)

Authority's decision on the issues

Peat extraction in County Fermanagh

In 1999 part of the drainage basin of the Cladagh River was leased by Fermanagh District Council and named the Cuilcagh Mountain Park. Commercial peat extraction was stopped and work began to restore the cutover area to bogland. The Environment and Heritage Service has introduced conservation measures under European environmental laws which protect the bogland. The Department of Agriculture and Rural Development (DARD) is working with farmers to ensure that farming does not damage the environment. The Marble Arch area is now a European GeoPark because of its special geological features. This gives it further protection.

Building an interpretive centre in the Burren, County Clare

In 1996 the OPW was instructed to restore the area by removing the car parks and building works and restoring the land to its original state. It applied for a scaled-down visitor centre, so the restoration was put on hold. In March 2000, planning permission for a visitor centre at Mullaghmore was turned down. In February 2001 the OPW was instructed to remove the car park (see photographs B and C on page 62), and restore the land to its original state (see photographs A and B below). The work was done by the same company responsible for the building work which was stopped in 1993. A new visitor centre has been built at Ballyvaughan, and the centre at Kilfenora has been rebuilt and upgraded.

Car park at Mullaghmore (2005)

The land restored to its original state

The Ballynahone bog issue in County Londonderry

Permission to extract peat was given in 1988, and drains were cut in 1991. A group known as the Friends of Ballynahone Bog was formed to oppose the peat company and they continued their opposition until 1994 when permission was withdrawn and the drains were filled in. In 1995 the site became an Area of Special Scientific Interest (ASSI) and was taken over by the government. This site has now been protected as a Special Area of Conservation (SAC) and as a National Nature Reserve (NNR). In 2000, the Ulster Wildlife Trust (UWT) took over management of the site in conjunction with the Friends of Ballynahone Bog and the Environment and Heritage Service.

THEME E

Economic Change and Development

This theme deals with economic change in both developed and developing areas of the world. It examines industrial location and change and some of the reasons put forward to account for uneven economic development. It provides an opportunity to examine both environmental and development issues.

Economic activity

Any activity, industry or job which makes money is an economic activity.
Economic activities can be divided into three types.

1 Primary industries

These obtain the raw materials we need from the Earth. These jobs include farming, mining and quarrying.

2 Secondary industries

These take the raw material and make it into something useful. These jobs include most manufacturing industries and factories such as shipbuilding, car assembly and food processing.

3 Tertiary industries

These provide a service to other industries. These jobs include transport, retailing and wholesaling, advertising, communications, and design of packaging.

1.1 Change in function of industrial premises

Economic activities and industries are continually changing. They can move to a new site, expand, contract or close. Changes in industry may result in unemployment, but they can create new opportunities. New industries can move in or land can be freed for new development. We will look at three case studies where economic change has led to new opportunities.

Case study Yorkgate

In the York Street area of Belfast there has been a major change of land use. The land was occupied by a large cigarette factory owned by Gallaher. Changing smoking habits and a loss of markets meant that the factory was no longer needed, and it was closed in 1988. The site is in an excellent position for retailing and services and was redeveloped as Yorkgate in 1991. This is an example of a brownfield site which can be redeveloped and have its land use changed. Using brownfield sites like this saves greenfield sites where farming land is built over. Gallaher provided 1000 secondary jobs. These have been replaced by 300–350 tertiary jobs.

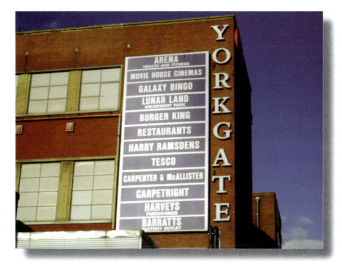

Case study Andrews' Mill, Comber

In 1918 Northern Ireland had over 200 industries connected with linen production, employing over 90 000 people. By 2005 these numbers had reduced to 15 industries employing around 1500 people. One result of this was the closure of many factories, which were either demolished or changed their use. At one stage Andrews' Mill in Comber provided over 850 jobs for local people. When it closed in 1997 the site became available for redevelopment. The following ideas were considered:

- Shopping complex
- Small business units
- Town houses
- Upmarket flats and apartments

Andrews' Mill, Comber, Co Down

Eventually it was decided to go for the last option and over the last two years the mill has gradually been converted into flats and apartments. Houses have been built in the grounds. The prices range from £165 000 to £250 000 and are well beyond the budget of local people. They are aimed at people with well-paid jobs 9 miles away in Belfast who want to live within easy commuting distance. The complex includes a lake, a millstream, landscaped grounds and courtyards, a fitness suite, private swimming pool, spa, broadband internet access, and 24-hour security on site. It is also hi-fi ready – the speakers are already in place!

Case study Changing land use – Watertop Farm

New opportunities also occur in a primary industry. It has happened in Northern Ireland recently with many farmers considering diversification. This means looking at other ways to bring in income to the farm. This can mean growing other crops, but sometimes it involves some aspect of leisure or recreation – a tertiary or service activity. Diversification includes:

- A golf course
- A driving range
- Pony trekking
- Bed & Breakfast
- Farm holidays

Resource A ▶

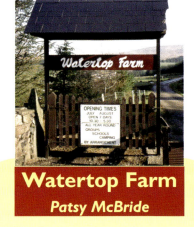

Many farms have become open farms – they open the farm to the public and offer a range of activities designed to bring in extra income. These include tours of the farm and opportunities to watch what happens on the farm. There are now over 20 open farms in Northern Ireland including Watertop Farm near Ballycastle in County Antrim (see the photograph above).

Resource A shows the main features of Watertop Farm. It is a hill sheep farm very like Dieskirt Farm on page 22.

Watertop Farm
Patsy McBride

Location	Watertop
Nearest town	Ballycastle, 8 km
Height above sea level	150–330 metres
Soil	One-third loam on till, two-thirds peat
Size	Total land area 262 ha (244 ha + 18 rented)
Crops	Grass 25% Rough grazing 75%
Livestock	
Dairy cattle	None
Beef cattle	30
Sheep	650 made up of 175 Scottish Blackface, 120 Cheviots and 355 cross breeds. These will give over 800 lambs.
Labour	1 + 1 part time
Main products & market	Lambs and beef cattle to market at Ballycastle, Ballymoney or Ballyvoy
Diversification	Open farm (since 1986)

The farm still functions as a working hill farm but now offers a wide range of activities as well – see Resource B. Resource C shows the change this has made to the farm income.

Resource B

- Pony trekking
- Trout fishing
- Boating
- Pony rides
- Farm tours
- Sheep shearing
- Tearoom and shop
- Museum
- Touring caravans and camping
- Outdoor activities, eg archery, abseiling, rope course and team building
- School visits
- Fieldwork

A school visiting the farm museum

Farm income

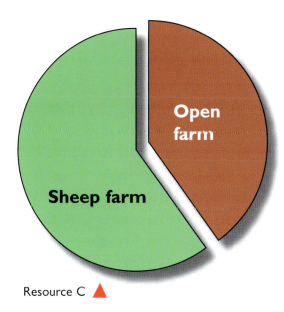

Resource C ▲

Government/EU assistance

The link between subsidies and production has been removed. This is called **decoupling.** This means the farmer no longer needs to produce in order to receive subsidy. However, land must be kept in good agricultural and environmental condition.

- From 2005 many of the previous subsidy schemes will be replaced with a Single Farm Payment. This is made up of two parts:
    - An area component of approximately £48 per hectare
    - A historic component based on average subsidy claims in the years 2000–02
- Producers farming in Less Favoured Areas (LFAs) will continue to be eligible to receive the Less Favoured Area Compensatory Allowance (LFACA).
- Other payments are made to farmers who participate in agri-environment programmes, under which they agree to abide by certain conditions aimed at delivering environmental improvements, eg Countryside Management Scheme (CMS) and Environmentally Sensitive Areas (ESAs).

Tearoom and shop

School groups tour the farm in this ex-army lorry

Boating/fishing lake

1.2 Factors of location of hi-tech industry

Case study   Industrial location

Industrial location is the reason why an industry locates in a particular place. Northern Ireland used to be a favourable location for traditional industries such as linen, shipbuilding, engineering and textiles but these have declined and provide fewer jobs. Government, councils and Invest Northern Ireland are keen to replace these jobs with newer industries. The newer industries are often quaternary industries (research and development) based on high technology, computers and software. These industries do not have the restriction of older industries as to where they locate. They are free to locate wherever they like. An industry which is not tied to a particular place and can locate anywhere is called a footloose industry.

Traditional industries were tied to certain locations. A linen mill needed water for power and spinning, a steelworks had to be close to bulky raw materials like coal and iron ore, and a car assembly plant had to be in an urban area near its market. Modern hi-tech industries are not tied like this. Resource D shows the locational factors for new industries which have located in the Antrim Technology Park in Northern Ireland. This is a purpose-built area, specially designed to attract the newer hi-tech industries.

Resource D

Raw materials
Few raw materials needed, or light raw materials which would be easy to import

Government or EU assistance
Invest NI can provide up to 20% of start-up costs. It also helps by giving advice and support for new businesses about grants, recruitment and training, research and development, marketing, pre-employment training, and using ICT.

Labour
A well educated workforce in the local area

Power
Electricity from the local grid

Site
32 hectare woodland setting with units up to 1750 m²

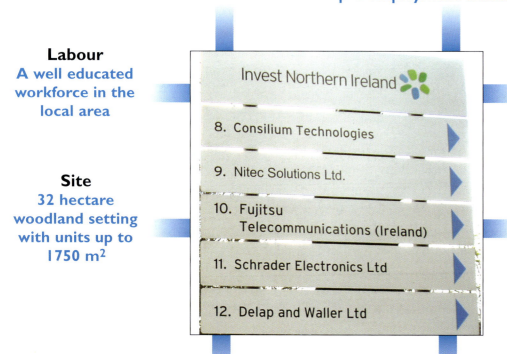

Market
Easy access to UK and Europe, but the internet can be used to reach a global market

Transport
Belfast International Airport is only 5 km away, and the ports of Larne (32 km) and Belfast (24 km) are easily reached by a good road network via the nearby M2 motorway.

Technical support
The nearby universities at Belfast and Jordanstown can offer expert advice, support and research facilities to enable companies to keep up with the latest technological innovations.

3.1 Differences in development between MEDCs and LEDCs

Countries have different levels of economic development. Development can be measured using different indicators. The indicators show us the level of development in a country. Study Resource E which shows a selection of countries and some indicators.

Resource E ▼	Norway	UK	Brazil	South Africa	Kenya	Sierra Leone
GDP in $	41 974	26 444	2593	2299	393	150
Life expectancy (years)	79	78	68	51	46	35
Infant mortality (per 1000 live births)	4	5	30	52	78	165
% living on less than $1 per day	0	0	8	7	23	57
Mobile phones (per 1000 people)	844	841	201	304	37	14
United Nations Human Development Index (HDI)	1	12	72	119	148	177

3.2 Appropriate technology to encourage economic development

LEDCs have been receiving aid from MEDCs since the mid 1960s. Much of this aid has not been appropriate or sustainable. There are too many examples of multi-million-dollar projects that failed to deliver benefits to the LEDC concerned. Failures include:

Tied aid where the LEDC got the aid only if it bought goods or services from the MEDC, eg when Germany tarred the main roads in Sierra Leone providing that the government bought a fleet of Mercedes buses for the National Bus Company. Sierra Leone could not afford the petrol to run them or the price of spare parts and within a few years the buses were scrap. Sierra Leone was left to pay the debt.

Large projects which generated hydro electric power (HEP) for far-away cities, but left the local people no better off or even worse off because their farms and villages had been flooded to provide a dam, eg Aswan in Egypt. Aswan also suffered because the fertile silt was trapped behind the dam, and farmers downstream from the dam had to buy expensive imported artificial fertiliser.

Projects that were totally inappropriate for the country concerned, eg a steelworks in Zambia where there was no market for steel. The cost of making it was so high that it could not compete with cheaper products when they tried to export it.

Projects which failed to take account of world trade conditions, eg when Ghana borrowed money for an irrigation scheme to help local farmers grow tomatoes. When the farmers went to sell their tomatoes in the market they found that EU tomatoes were for sale at a cheaper price as the EU paid subsidies to European farmers and they could sell their tomatoes in Ghana cheaper than the local tomatoes.

Projects that were downright dangerous, eg when the Philippines borrowed money to build a nuclear power station on a fault line in an earthquake zone. The power station never opened but the debt had to be repaid.

The result of these and many other similar schemes is that by 1980 the global debt of all LEDCs was $567 billion. By 1992 the debt had increased to $1.4 trillion. In these 12 years countries concerned paid back in interest three times the original debt they owed. The debt itself remained. Poor countries now pay over $50 million **every day.** As a result of this problem many charities and Non-Governmental Organisations (NGOs) are looking to Appropriate or Intermediate Technology that is less expensive, more environmentally friendly and sustainable. They are also campaigning for an end to third world debt.

Appropriate or Intermediate Technology tries to match the project to the need of the local people. How can we help farmers in East Africa without tying them in to diesel and spares for a £30 000 tractor? Resource F shows an example.

Resource F ▼

Farmers in East Africa break up the soil using hand tools or digging sticks.

The Appropriate or Intermediate solution is to provide them with steel-bladed ploughs pulled by local oxen.

Farmers in Northern Ireland break up the soil using the latest hi-tech machinery.

This is better than what they have now but avoids the drawbacks of the hi-tech solution. A further advantage is that the money you would spend on one modern tractor would buy 100 plough-and-oxen teams.

FAO/12400/F. Mattioli

Case study
Water pump as you play

One of the biggest needs in an LEDC is a reliable supply of clean fresh water. Water-borne diseases are killers in LEDCs.

Interesting Fact

- Each person needs 50 litres of clean water per day.
- In the UK we use an average of 200 litres per day.
- Each year 5–10 million people die as a result of poor quality water.
- 80% of diseases in LEDCs result from polluted water and unhygienic sanitation.

Once again we have to strike a balance between getting water from a river or waterhole, which is open to animals and livestock, and providing a supply of clean piped water such as our own in Northern Ireland. In many LEDCs there is clean fresh water in the rocks underground – the problem is in pumping it to the surface. The hi-tech solution is a diesel powered pump that needs fuel, expertise and parts. In one area of South Africa they have found a better solution. Look at Resources G and H.

Resource G ▶

Roundabout Outdoor

Resource H ▼

Roundabout Outdoor

The children of the village pump the water to the tank as they play on the roundabout. Every turn of the roundabout pumps 4 litres of water into the tank. The pump can deliver 1400 litres of water per hour from a depth of 40 metres. The tank holds 2500 litres. This is better than getting water from a river but it does not require the money and expertise to run a diesel pump.

It is appropriate and sustainable for the following reasons:

- The pump only has two moving parts.
- It can be easily fixed by training a local engineer.
- It does not use expensive imported fuel.
- The cost of the pump roundabout is £4400 and advertising sold on the tanks pays for maintenance, making the whole system sustainable, into the future.
- It uses renewable energy!
- The local village now has a year-round supply of clean, fresh water.
- The children no longer suffer from water-borne diseases like cholera, worms, bilharzias, diarrhoea and dysentery.
- Money is being saved on health care and this can be used in other areas of the village.
- Women are freed from the daily chore of collecting water. Many of them had to walk several kilometres to a river and then carry 20 litres of water home on their heads (this weighs the same as 4 bags of potatoes).

Over 400 of these pumps have been installed in South Africa and they are providing water for around 200 000 people.

3.3 Fair trade

Case study Fairtrade

There are many reasons for this pattern of development. One of the main reasons is unfair trading patterns between MEDCs and LEDCs. Farmers in LEDCs sometimes do not get paid very much for their crop. In the last 13 years an organisation called the Fairtrade Foundation has tried to do something to improve the standard of living for farmers in LEDCs.

Resource 1 shows the value of Fairtrade products.

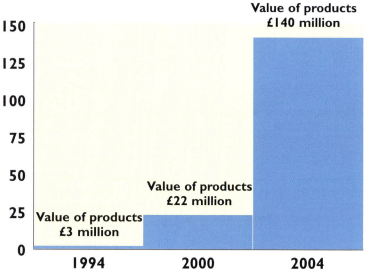

The FAIRTRADE Mark shows consumers that the farmers benefit from a better deal.

Resource 1 ▲

There are over 800 Fairtrade products on sale in the UK. Internationally, they are produced in 49 LEDCs, benefiting over 5 million people. Fairtrade means:

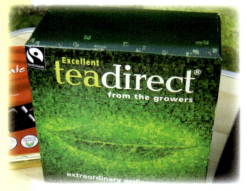

- Farmers receive a fair price for their products. In October 2001 the world price for coffee was 45 cents per pound. Fairtrade was paying their suppliers 121 cents per pound. See Resource J overleaf.

- Farmers receive a stable price for their product. The price does not fluctuate in a short space of time.

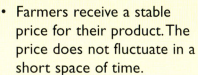

- Farmers have an opportunity to improve their lives.

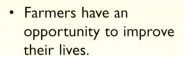

- There is a greater respect for the environment.

- Small-scale farmers have a stronger position in world markets.

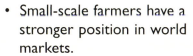

- There is a closer link between consumers and producers.

- A premium (extra payment) is paid to help community development.

Resource J

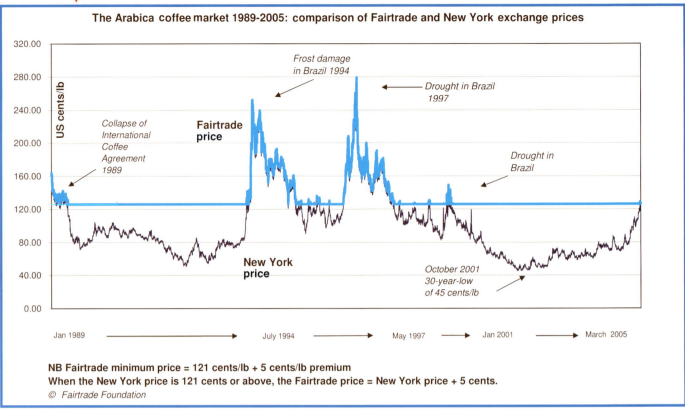

The Arabica coffee market 1989-2005: comparison of Fairtrade and New York exchange prices

Collapse of International Coffee Agreement 1989

Frost damage in Brazil 1994

Drought in Brazil 1997

Fairtrade price

Drought in Brazil

New York price

October 2001 30-year-low of 45 cents/lb

Jan 1989 — July 1994 — May 1997 — Jan 2001 — March 2005

NB Fairtrade minimum price = 121 cents/lb + 5 cents/lb premium
When the New York price is 121 cents or above, the Fairtrade price = New York price + 5 cents.
© *Fairtrade Foundation*

- After oil, coffee is the second most valuable commodity.
- Britain spends £730 million per year on coffee.
- In the UK we drink 70 million cups per day.
- On average that is 1.5 cups per person per day.
- Fairtrade coffee sales approached £50 million in 2004.

Northern Ireland is the last link in a long chain. The products originate in tropical countries and end up on the shelves of supermarkets in Northern Ireland. Non-Governmental Organisations (NGOs) such as War on Want (Northern Ireland), Oxfam, Traidcraft and Tear Fund support the Fairtrade Foundation and market the products in Northern Ireland. They also campaign for supermarkets to stock fair trade products and encourage local councils to use Fairtrade tea and coffee.

There are big advantages for farmers. We get more money for our crops. We didn't make enough money to live on before. Now we get a better price and the money comes directly to us. I can buy more food, I can help support my daughter at university, and I can take care of my son.

Questions

1 Study Resource K which shows a diagram of the playpump, and answer the questions which follow.

Resource K ▶

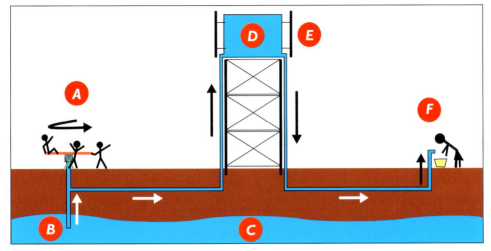

(a) Match up the following features with the correct letter from the diagram.

Billboards	…
Tap	…
Borehole	…
Roundabout	…
Ground water	…
Tank	…

(6)

(b) Give two reasons why this playpump is sustainable. (4)

(c) State and explain two ways in which this playpump is a better investment than a diesel-powered pump.
(6)

2 Study the OS map of Marble Arch on page 64, and then copy and complete the following table to show whether the feature shown is primary, secondary or tertiary. (5)

Grid reference	Economic activity
180345	
168304	
170330	
121345	
112368	

3 Study the photograph on the right which shows a Fairtrade product on sale in a local supermarket.

(a) Name the product shown in the photograph. (1)

(b) State and explain one reason why the farmer who produces this product will benefit by belonging to a Fairtrade Co-operative. (3)

Settlements and Change

This theme concentrates on the situation and location of settlements, their distribution within a landscape, and their internal structure. Settlements are synoptic features of the environment which grow and decay through processes such as urbanisation and counterurbanisation. Planning has a major impact on settlements.

1.1 Physical and economic site factors related to the location and growth of settlements

A settlement is a place where people live. It can vary from an isolated dwelling or farmhouse to a city the size of Mexico City with more than 20 million people. All settlements had small beginnings of one or two houses. Some have stayed small, others have grown slightly, while others have grown into very large settlements.

Settlements in Northern Ireland grew up in various places for the following reasons:

- **Defensive site**
  The Normans picked places which could be easily defended by building a castle, eg Carrickfergus, Dundrum.

- **Route centre**
  Where two or more roads crossed, a settlement would grow up, eg Dungannon, Ballymena, Lisburn.

Carrickfergus – defensive site

Ballymena – route centre

- **Bridging point**
  This was where a river could easily be crossed with a ford and later a bridge, eg Banbridge, Omagh, Enniskillen.

- **Lowest bridging point**
  This was the bridging point closest to the mouth of a river and was the last place to cross a river before it reached the sea, eg Belfast, Coleraine, Derry.

Omagh – bridging point

- **Highest point of navigation/port**
  This was the furthest point that ships could go inland. If the ships could not go any further then they had to unload and a port developed. This usually coincided with the lowest bridging point, eg Belfast, Coleraine, Derry.

- **Water supply**
  A supply of fresh water was essential. Water is needed on a daily basis and the people who

Belfast – lowest bridging point and highest point of navigation/port

lived in the settlement would not want to have to go too far to obtain fresh water.

People also had to be able to grow food, and keep animals nearby, so flat land was useful. They also needed wood for building and fuel. Until the seventeenth century what is now Northern Ireland was covered with trees and finding wood was not a problem.

If a settlement had more than one of these features then it was more likely to grow and develop. A settlement which was only a route centre would stay small whereas a settlement which had all six features would be attractive to people and would grow and attract more people. Many towns in Northern Ireland are both route centres and bridging points so they have become larger settlements, eg Omagh, Enniskillen, Ballymena, Downpatrick, and Portadown. Derry and Belfast had all six features while Coleraine and Newry had five. Once a settlement is bigger than its neighbours, then it provides more jobs and services which attract more people and it continues to grow. This growth of towns and cities is called urbanisation.

Case study   The site and location of Belfast

What attracted people to the site of Belfast, why did they settle there and why did Belfast grow to be the largest town in Northern Ireland and the second largest in Ireland? Resource A shows the site of Belfast. It was built on a sandbank where the Farset River flowed into the Lagan. It also shows the location of Belfast.

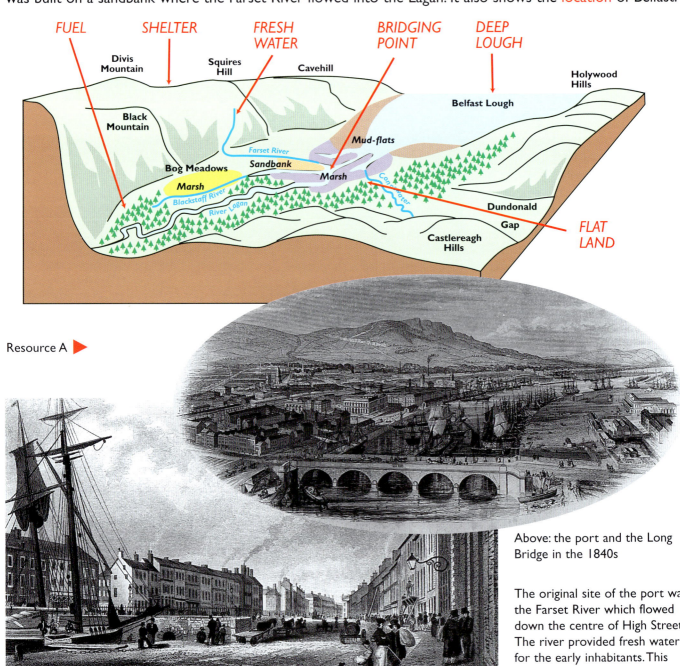

Resource A ▶

Above: the port and the Long Bridge in the 1840s

The original site of the port was the Farset River which flowed down the centre of High Street. The river provided fresh water for the early inhabitants. This 1831 painting shows the Farset before it was covered over when ships became too big to use it.

Case study   Urbanisation, the growth of Belfast

Belfast remained reasonably small until the early nineteenth century. In 1815 it had a population of 30 000. This would have made it bigger than present day Newtownards but smaller than Ballymena. In the next 150 years there was rapid urbanisation. This is shown by Resource B.

Resource B ▼

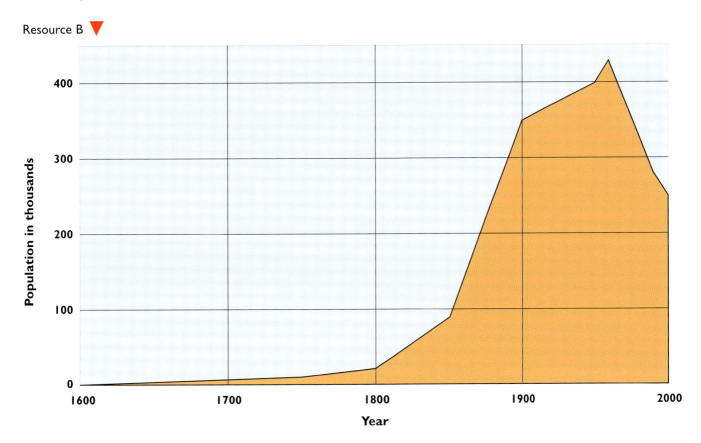

This growth cannot be explained by birth rates and death rates alone. The majority of this growth came as a result of migration. In the nineteenth century people moved into Belfast from all over Ulster. This is called rural–urban migration. In MEDCs it took place in the nineteenth century, in LEDCs it took place in the late twentieth century. This movement was governed by push–pull factors. Push factors are what pushes people from where they live. Pull factors are what attracts people to where they want to go. There is usually a barrier to movement of people by migration. In many cases this is a combination of distance and cost. Resource C shows some of the push–pull factors which operated in nineteenth-century Belfast.

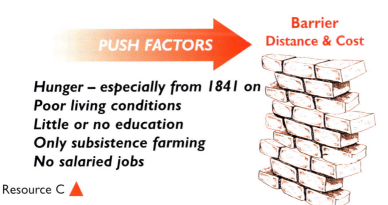

PUSH FACTORS

Barrier
Distance & Cost

PULL FACTORS

Hunger – especially from 1841 on
Poor living conditions
Little or no education
Only subsistence farming
No salaried jobs

Jobs in cotton or linen mills
*   from 1810 on*
Better houses rented out by
*   mill owners*
Chance of education in urban schools
Salaried jobs

Resource C ▲

The growth of Belfast outstripped other settlements and it became the largest city in the north of Ireland. It is still the largest city in Northern Ireland although in the second half of the twentieth century the population declined.

Case study Counterurbanisation: the decline of Belfast

Counterurbanisation is the name given to the movement of people out of large urban areas like Belfast. This movement is more common in cities in MEDCs. There are a number of reasons why counterurbanisation takes place, but like urbanisation they are governed by push–pull factors as shown in Resource D.

Barrier

PUSH FACTORS

*Higher levels of pollution
Traffic problems and danger to children
Older houses
Small gardens
Problems caused by the Troubles
No open space or play areas*

PULL FACTORS

*Cleaner environment
Less traffic and safer for children
Newer houses
Larger gardens
Less impact from the Troubles
Close to countryside and green fields*

Resource D ▲

Many people moved out of Belfast in the 1960s and 1970s when the inner city areas were redeveloped. Movement occurred in three ways:
- To large estates on the edge of the city, eg Rathcoole, Braniel, Belvoir, or Ballymurphy
- To growth towns in the Greater Belfast area, eg Bangor, Lisburn or Antrim
- To commuter villages in the green belt, eg Ballynure, Moneyreagh, Ballygowan or Crumlin (see page 126)
The maps (Resources E and F) show some of these places.

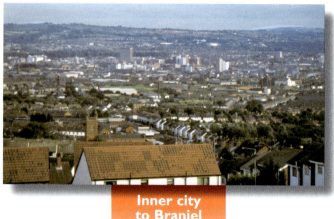

Inner city to Braniel

From Belfast to Crumlin

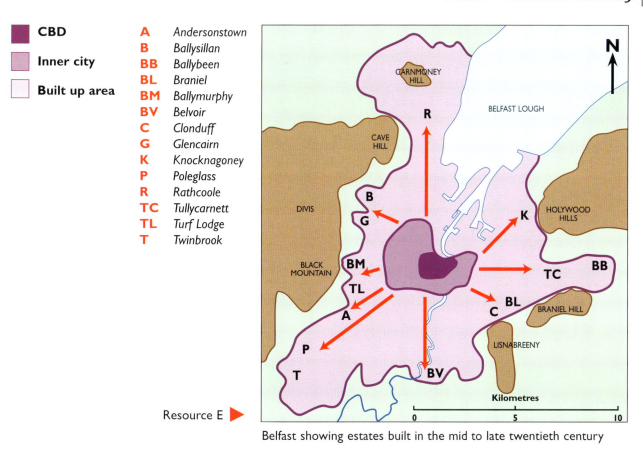

CBD

Inner city

Built up area

A	*Andersonstown*
B	*Ballysillan*
BB	*Ballybeen*
BL	*Braniel*
BM	*Ballymurphy*
BV	*Belvoir*
C	*Clonduff*
G	*Glencairn*
K	*Knocknagoney*
P	*Poleglass*
R	*Rathcoole*
TC	*Tullycarnett*
TL	*Turf Lodge*
T	*Twinbrook*

Resource E ▶

Belfast showing estates built in the mid to late twentieth century

Resource F ▼   Greater Belfast showing towns and commuter villages

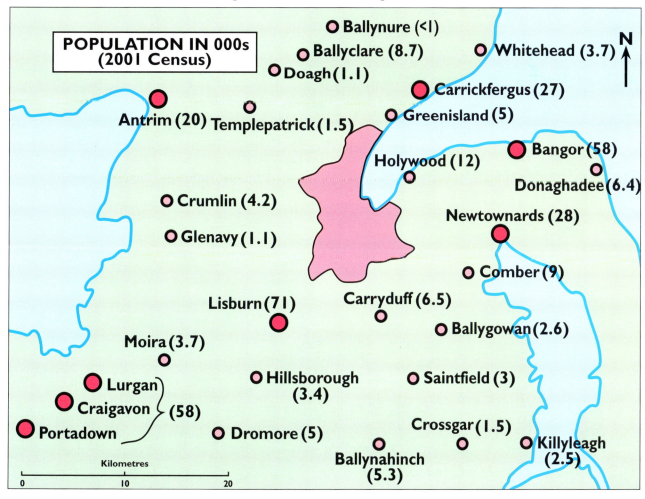

**POPULATION IN 000s
(2001 Census)**

Ballynure (<1)
Ballyclare (8.7)
Whitehead (3.7)
Doagh (1.1)
Carrickfergus (27)
Antrim (20) Templepatrick (1.5)
Greenisland (5)
Holywood (12)
Bangor (58)
Donaghadee (6.4)
Crumlin (4.2)
Newtownards (28)
Glenavy (1.1)
Comber (9)
Lisburn (71)
Carryduff (6.5)
Ballygowan (2.6)
Moira (3.7)
Lurgan
Hillsborough (3.4)
Saintfield (3)
Craigavon (58)
Portadown
Dromore (5)
Crossgar (1.5)
Killyleagh (2.5)
Ballynahinch (5.3)

Counterurbanisation is still taking place today and many of these villages and towns are now much bigger than they once were. In 1960 Comber had less than 3000 people; counterurbanisation from Belfast led to a population of 9000 by 2001. There are plans for a further 650 houses which would push the population towards 12 000 by 2010. This leads to conflict between older residents and newcomers. This is shown in Resource G.

Resource G ▶

Against increasing the size of the village

- Everybody knows everybody else in the village.
- We don't want a lot of newcomers from Belfast.
- There will be more traffic and the children will be at more risk.
- Petty crime and vandalism are bound to increase.
- We will lose the village atmosphere that we have.
- We will become a commuter settlement.

For increasing the size of the village

- The shops will get more trade.
- The school will get more pupils.
- You can't live in the past – you have to make progress.
- We can attract jobs and services that we don't have.
- The council will get more money from the rates so that they can improve facilities.

Ballynure is 20 km from Belfast. The original village is being supplemented with new houses.

Moneyreagh is 9 km from Belfast. It has a new shopping area as well as many new houses.

1.2 Settlement hierarchy

A hierarchy is a method by which settlements are put in order of size. This ranges from a city at the top to an isolated house/farm at the bottom. This ordering is done on a combination of three factors:

1 The population of the settlement
2 The services provided by the settlement
3 The population density of the settlement

Resource H shows a settlement hierarchy for Northern Ireland.
It is based on population figures for the 2001 census.

Resource H ▶

Settlement hierarchy
for Northern Ireland
(population in thousands)
Source: 2001 NI Census

Settlements become bigger in population

Settlements become fewer in number

CITIES (2)
Greater
Belfast 394,
Derry 83

LARGE TOWNS (11)
Lisburn 71, Bangor 58,
Craigavon 58, Ballymena 29,
Newtownards 28, Newry 27,
Carrickfergus 27, Coleraine 24,
Antrim 20, Omagh 20, Larne 18

MEDIUM TOWNS (9)
Banbridge 14.7, Armagh 14.5, Enniskillen 13.5,
Strabane 13.3, Limavady 12, Holywood 12,
Dungannon 11, Cookstown 10.5, Downpatrick 10.3

SMALL TOWNS (17)
Ballymoney 9, Comber 9, Ballyclare 8.7, Magherafelt 8.2,
Portstewart 7.8, Newcastle 7.4, Warrenpoint 6.9, Carryduff 6.5,
Donaghadee 6.4, Kilkeel 6.3, Portrush 6.3, Ballynahinch 5.3, Ballycastle 5,
Greenlsland 5, Dromore (Down) 5, Randalstown 4.9, Coalisland 4.8

INTERMEDIATE SETTLEMENTS (24)
Crumlin 4.2, Whitehead 3.7, Moira 3.7, Maghera 3.6, Hillsborough 3.4,
Eglinton 3.1, Ahoghill 3, Tandragee 3, Dungiven 3, Saintfield 3, Keady 2.9, Culmore 2.9,
Richhill 2.8, Castlederg 2.7, Lisnaskea 2.7, Ballygowan 2.6, Waringstown 2.5, Killyleagh 2.5,
New Buildings 2.5, Portaferry 2.4, Rostrevor 2.4, Cullybackey 2.4, Castlewellan 2.3, Broughshane 2.3

VILLAGES (51)
Castledawson 2, Sion Mills 2, Rathfriland 2, Dollingstown 1.8, Ballykelly 1.8, Irvinestown 1.8,
Millisle 1.8, Annalong 1.7, Kells 1.7, Maghaberry 1.7, Ardglass 1.6, Draperstown 1.6, Portavogie 1.6,
Strathfoyle 1.6, Templepatrick 1.5, Gilford 1.5, Crossgar 1.5, Kilrea 1.5, Newtownstewart 1.4, Crossmaglen 1.4,
Carnlough 1.4, Ballywalter 1.4, Moneymore 1.4, Helen's Bay 1.3, Fintona 1.3, Ballinamallard 1.3, Castlerock 1.3,
Claudy 1.3, Bushmills 1.3, Markethill 1.3, Garvagh 1.3, Drumaness 1.2, Cushendall 1.2, Cloughmills 1.2, Greysteel 1.2,
Kircubbin 1.2, Moy 1.2, Portglenone 1.2, Fivemiletown 1.1, Dromore (Tyrone) 1.1, Magheralin 1.1, Annahilt 1.1, Doagh 1.1,
Bellaghy 1.1, Glenavy 1.1, Seahill 1.1, Cogry/Kilbride 1.1, Dundrum 1.1, Dunloy 1, Lisbellaw 1, Greyabbey 1

Hamlets (Too numerous to mention!)

Belfast Metropolitian Area:
This includes North Down, Castlereagh, Lisburn, Newtownabbey and Carrickfergus
council areas. It has a total population of 580 000.
The Derry Urban Area has a total population of 91 000.

Case study The urban field of Ballymena

Urban field/sphere of influence

Each settlement in the settlement hierarchy draws people into it from the surrounding area. Villages will draw people in to shop from 5 or 6 kilometres at the most. Cities will draw people in from 100 kilometres for some services. This area is called the urban field or sphere of influence of the settlement. That is the area round the settlement from which people will travel to that settlement for goods and services. It is possible to map the area around a settlement and draw a line on a map to show the urban field. This can be worked out using a combination of the following methods:

- Questionnaire – find out where the people who shop in the settlement live.
- Local newspaper – find out the area covered by the local newspaper.
- Local schools – find out where the local school draws its pupils from.
- Bus routes – find out which nearby settlements are served by buses.
- Council boundary – for larger settlements, find out the area covered by the local council.
- Shops – find out the area that local shops or food takeaways will deliver to.

Resource 1 shows the urban field of Ballymena using a shopping questionnaire, local newspaper, school catchment and council boundary.

Resource 1 ▼

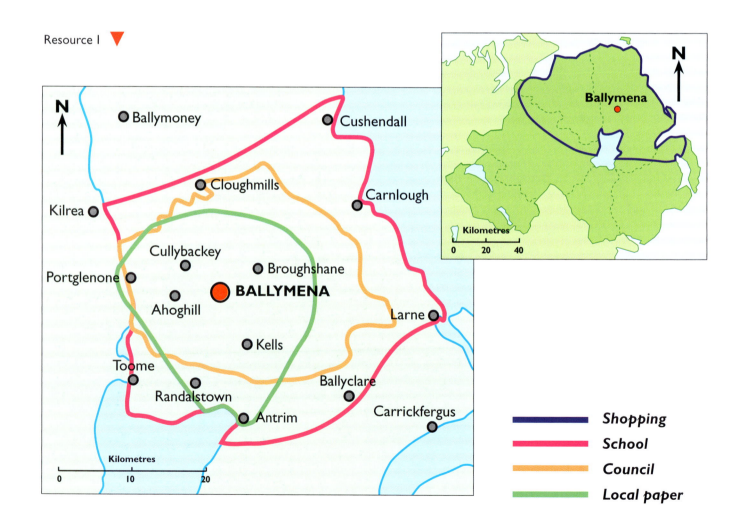

Shopping
School
Council
Local paper

2.2 Characteristics of and contrasts in locations of CBD, industrial zones, residential zones and green belt

Case study Functional zones/land use zones

All settlements have functional zones where most of the land has the same use or function. Villages will consist mainly of houses and a small commercial/shopping area. Hamlets will be all houses. Large towns and cities will have more of these zones and they will cover a greater area. The main zones are as follows:

Belfast's CBD

- **Central Business District (CBD):**
  This is an area of shops, offices, businesses, entertainment, multi-storey car parks, chain stores and shopping arcades. It may have a pedestrian zone in the centre and may also contain a town hall, city hall or guild hall. The headquarters of banks, building societies and insurance companies may be found there.

- **Industrial zones:**
  These are areas of industries and factories.

Belfast docks

- **Residential zones:**
  These are areas of housing of different types. This zone can be sub-divided by housing type or by age.

Botanic Gardens, Belfast

Residential street in Belfast

- **Recreation zones:**
  These are areas which are set aside for recreation and leisure. They include playing fields, parks, leisure centres and golf courses.

• **Transport zones:**
These are areas set aside for transport use. They include car parks, bus stations, railway stations, goods yards and airports.

Left: Belfast City Airport, Sydenham

• **Public buildings:**
These are usually dotted around in other zones, but sometimes they take up a large amount of land and form a zone.
They include government offices, hospitals, churches, schools and police stations. Large cities are more likely to have these zones than smaller settlements. Belfast has a large zone of education in and around Queen's University, and a large zone of government offices around Stormont.

Above: Queen's University, Belfast

Left: Parliament Buildings, Stormont, Dundonald

Newtownards Town Hall

In large cities these land use zones can form a pattern. The pattern for Belfast is shown in Resource J.

Resource J ▶

Diagram of Hoyt's ring and sector model for Belfast

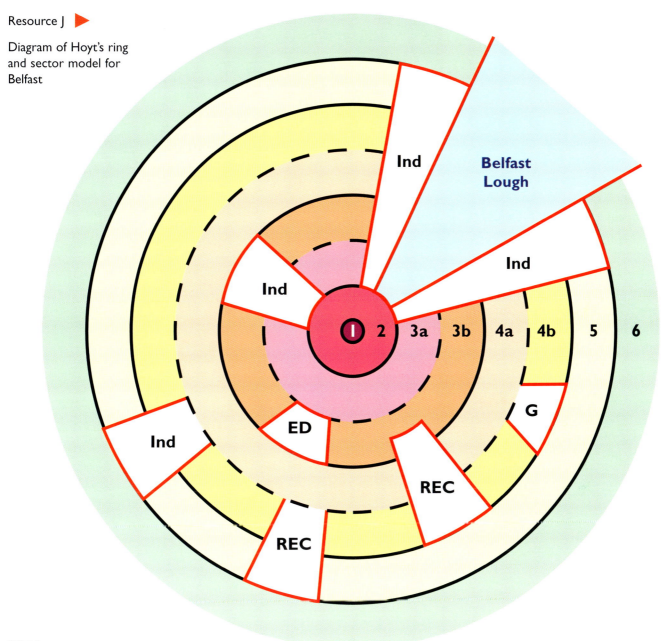

KEY

1   CBD
2   Twilight zone
3a   Inner city – late 19th century
3b   Inner city – early 20th century
4a   Outer city – pre-1945
4b   Outer city – post-1950
5   Suburbs – includes post-war housing estates
    and industrial estates
6   Green belt

ED   Education
REC   Recreation
G   Government
Ind   Industry

As you can see from the diagram, housing takes up the biggest area in all settlements. As settlements expand, different types of housing grow up. This can have positive (good) effects and negative (bad) effects on the population of the settlement.

CBD

This is the central area of Belfast (photograph A). It includes the main shopping areas and many of the businesses. The tallest buildings are found here as it is cheaper to build up rather than out. Land is at a premium and is expensive. This is the part of the city that is accessible to all, and the main roads and bus routes meet here. Buildings include the main Council offices in the City Hall (photograph B), multi-storey car parks (photograph C), large shopping malls (photograph D), and high-rise buildings which rent out office space (photograph E). There are large pedestrian zones to make shopping easier and more pleasant (photograph F).

Twilight zone

Twilight is a mixture of day and night. The twilight zone is a mixture of different land uses; this is how it gets its name. In the twilight zone you find a mixture of shops, offices, businesses, houses and transport. The twilight zone has been extensively redeveloped in Belfast. Photograph G shows a new office block in Victoria Street while photograph H shows a mixture of parking, houses, businesses and factories at Bridge End.

Inner city

This is the area that was built up in the nineteenth century to house the thousands of migrants flocking into Belfast for jobs. The houses are in terraces and were built with a yard at the back and an outside toilet. Many were 'two-up two-down' and they had no gardens and narrow streets as there were no cars. They were crammed as close together as possible so that more people could live in a small area. This type of housing is known as high density

housing. Photograph I shows an area of older housing in the Newtownards Road. Photograph J shows what has happened to large areas of inner-city Belfast, the older houses having been replaced with more modern housing with small gardens and provision for cars. These areas are built with a much lower density. A street of 80 houses can be replaced with 40, and the remaining families move out to newer estates in the suburbs or outer city (see page 125). Large areas have been redeveloped like this while other areas have been renovated.

Photographs K and L show the next stage – houses built in the early twentieth century which are a bit better than the houses in the inner city. They are still in terraces, but have small gardens and three storeys. The toilet would be inside and they would also have had a bathroom.

Outer city

These are houses built in the 1920s, 1930s and 1950s. The bulk of them are red-brick, semi-detached and have a much bigger garden and space for a garage. Photographs M and N show typical examples from west and south Belfast.

Suburbs

This is the area on the outskirts of the city. It includes detached and semi-detached houses, bungalows and chalet bungalows. They are low density with gardens and garages (photograph O). They were built in the mid to late twentieth century

as the city expanded. The suburbs also contain housing estates built to house the overflow from the redeveloped inner cities. These were usually built in the 1960s or 1970s, such as Braniel in photograph P.

Green belt

This is the area around a settlement which has very strict building controls. These were brought in during the 1960s and 1970s when it was feared that large settlements would keep growing and swallow up the surrounding villages and towns. Belfast has already expanded and surrounded the villages of Ballyhackamore, Newtownbreda, Finaghy, Dunmurry and Dundonald. These are now part of the suburbs of Belfast. In order to limit future growth, no planning permission is given for housing on greenfield sites. Developers are encouraged to use brownfield sites in the

city, such as the redeveloped areas around the River Lagan. (See case study on page 135). Photograph Q shows the green belt in Dundonald. Houses have been built right up to the stop line where development is allowed.

Industrial zones

These are areas reserved for factories and businesses. They are usually near the docks or on the cheaper land in the suburbs. They have purpose-built units, good transport links and are not close to houses so

that there are no complaints about traffic and noise. Photographs R and S show the industrial estate at Duncrue Street which is close to the docks for ease of import and export, and right beside the M2 motorway (photograph T) for easy transport of goods around Northern Ireland.

3.1 Measures to regenerate and improve inner cities

Case study Laganside

As urban areas become larger there is an increasing need for planning. Planners developed green belts to restrict the growth of towns. Planners were also responsible for clearing the sub-standard inner-city areas and replacing them with newer low density houses. The new estates on the edges of Belfast were also planned, as were the industrial estates designed to keep factories and houses apart. In the twenty-first century very few changes to a settlement can be made without permission from the planners. Some plans are on a small scale such as traffic calming measures in a street. Other plans are on a large scale such as the Laganside plan to completely redevelop the area alongside the River Lagan in Belfast.

The area around the River Lagan used to be the heart of Belfast – see Resource A on page 122. By the 1980s the area had become derelict for the following reasons:
- In the 1960s the main port area moved downstream to deeper water as the larger ships could no longer come up to the Queen's Bridge.
- The river was tidal, and unsightly mudflats were exposed at low tide. In warm days in summer there was a 'rotten egg' smell.
- People and businesses moved away to more attractive areas on the edge of the city.

Belfast joined a long list of British cities (London, Manchester, Liverpool, Bristol and Glasgow), whose old dock areas were derelict wastelands. The solution in all of these cities was the same – an organisation was set up to coordinate the regeneration of the area, to fund the necessary changes, and to ensure that all the people and businesses interested in using the area followed the one plan. In Belfast the plan was launched by the Laganside Corporation in 1989. Look at Resource K overleaf which shows a map of the Laganside area.

1989

Tidal mudflats at Ravenhill Reach

1994 / £14 m

The Lagan Weir holds the water back so that the mudflats are covered.

Stage by stage over the last 15 years the Laganside Corporation has gradually transformed the area.

The first step was the building of the Lagan Weir. While this was being built the following measures were also put into place:
- Strict laws cleaned up the water coming down the Lagan and its tributaries so that it was less polluted.
- The sewage system was improved and upgraded.
- The river was dredged to remove the mud.

Water quality is measured on a four-point scale from A (excellent) to D (seriously polluted). The Lagan has improved from Grade D in 1991 to Grade A/B in 2005 and this has made the Laganside area more attractive. The river can be used for water sports and recreation. Land close to the river became attractive to live and work on, people and businesses moved in, and a spiral of growth began. With a cleaner, more attractive river, the Laganside Corporation began a series of building projects to transform the area.

M2

DOCK STREET

NORTH QUEEN STREET

WEST LINK

NELSON STREET

CORPORATION STREET

CLARENDON ROAD

BARROW SQUARE

QUEEN'S ISLAND

QUEEN'S ROAD

AIRPORT ROAD

CLARENDON DOCK

ABERCORN BASIN

ODYSSEY

SYDENHAM ROAD

SYDENHAM BY PASS

YORK STREET

CORPORATION SQ.

CATHEDRAL QUARTER

CROSS HARBOUR CORRIDOR

DONEGALL STREET

DUNBAR LINK

QUAY

DONEGALL

M3

LAGAN WEIR

QUEEN'S QUAY

DEE STREET

ISLAND STREET

BALLYMACARRETT ROAD

NORTH STREET

ROYAL AVENUE

HIGH STREET

LAGANSIDE BUS CENTRE

MIDDLEPATH STREET

BRIDGE END

NEWTOWNARDS ROAD

DONEGALL PLACE

VICTORIA STREET

CHICHESTER STREET

GREGG'S QUAY

LAGANVIEW

HOWDEN SIROCCO
(Eastbank)

SHORT STRAND

WELLINGTON PL

OXFORD STREET

RIVER LAGAN

CITY HALL

MAY STREET

LANYON PLACE

ST GEORGE'S MARKET

MAYS MEADOW

POTTINGER QUAY

ALBERTBRIDGE ROAD

HOWARD STREET

BEDFORD STREET

EAST BRIDGE STREET

CENTRAL STATION

ST GEORGE'S HARBOUR

RAVENHILL ROAD

CROMAC STREET

ORMEAU AVENUE

RAVENHILL REACH

DUBLIN ROAD

GASWORKS

DONEGALL PASS

← TO M1

ORMEAU ROAD

UNIVERSITY STREET

ORMEAU EMBANKMENT

RIVER LAGAN

July 1999

0   100   200   300   400 metres

Resource K   Map of Laganside

Cross harbour road/rail link

The new road bridge linked the M1 and M2 with the Sydenham Bypass. Through traffic was taken out of the CBD so there was less traffic congestion. Journey times were reduced by 10–15 minutes as traffic was now able to bypass the CBD. The bridge carries 75 000 vehicles per day on average. The new rail bridge linked all three parts of the rail network to one station and passengers no longer had to catch a bus to take them to the train for Larne.

1989

1997 / £65 m

This area used to be the scrap metal quay.

It has been replaced with the cross-harbour road/rail link.

Clarendon Dock

The area has been redeveloped as a mixture of business and housing. Organisations which have located here include Zurich Insurance, CCEA (examination board), Regus Office Services, Hamilton Shipping and Prudential Assurance's new call centre. The area has generated over 2500 jobs, many of them new.

Clarendon Dock

Lanyon Place

This was once the site of Belfast's Markets and Oxford Street Bus Station. It is now the site of the Waterfront Hall (£32 million), the Hilton Hotel (£21 million), and the headquarters of BT (£35 million) and Northbrook Technology (£21 million). The Lanyon Quay building (£20 million) overlooking the river is an exclusive mixed-use development that will combine a nightclub, ground floor restaurants and upper floor offices.

Oxford Street Bus Station, 1984

Lanyon Place, 2000

Gasworks area

This was the site of Belfast Gasworks, opened in 1823 and closed in 1988. The site had to be decontaminated as the soil was heavily polluted after 150 years of industrial use. Most of the soil was excavated and removed as it was too difficult and costly to clean. The site is now home to the Halifax Direct Internet Banking Building (£45 million) – a national call centre employing just under 2000 people. The 132-bedroom Radisson SAS Hotel opened here in September 2004, and other residents include the BBC and the Department for Social Development (DSD). A social housing scheme includes sheltered accommodation for the Chinese community. Three of the old buildings including the clock tower and the Klondyke building have been preserved as they are of architectural interest.

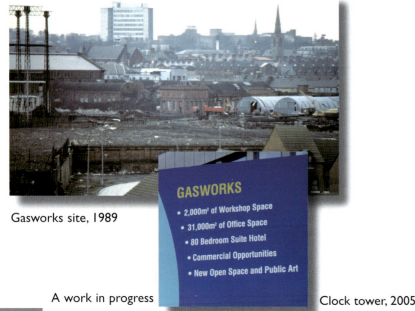

Gasworks site, 1989

GASWORKS
- 2,000m² of Workshop Space
- 31,000m² of Office Space
- 80 Bedroom Suite Hotel
- Commercial Opportunities
- New Open Space and Public Art

A work in progress

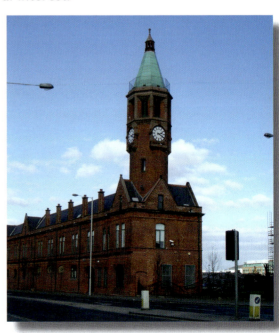

Clock tower, 2005

Abercorn Basin

This area has been developed by the Millennium Commission. The Odyssey Complex contains a 10 000-seater sports and concert arena, an IMAX cinema, a 12-screen multiplex cinema, the W5 Interactive Science Centre, and a range of shops, bars and restaurants.

1995

The Odyssey site in 1995

2001 / £90 m

The Odyssey, 2001

New housing

Gregg's Quay, 1989

Gregg's Quay, 2001

Ravenhill Reach, Gregg's Quay, Laganview, St George's Harbour, St John's Wharf and Queen's Quay are areas of new houses, apartments and flats fronting the river. In 2005 they are selling for £130 000–£300 000+ depending on the number of rooms. The big advantage for buyers, apart from the views over the river, is that they are within easy walking distance of the CBD with its shops, offices, businesses and entertainment. Further housing is planned for Donegall Quay. The Abbey Call Centre is at Mays Meadow and provides 650 jobs. New houses like these improve the socioeconomic class of the area. This is called gentrification.

Laganview, 2001

Cathedral Quarter

Central to this area is the historic St Anne's Cathedral. Laganside's vision is that this area will become a dynamic mixed-use cultural quarter – a home for the arts as well as cafes, bars, quality restaurants and commercial activity. Laganside has restored three old buildings – Cotton Court (Waring Street), Shah Din (Donegall Street) and the Northern Bank (Royal Avenue) – as Managed Workspace. Managed Workspace buildings provide affordable accommodation to a range of arts, craft and community groups. At the time of writing, work is due to start shortly on developments in Talbot Street car park and the Four Corners site on the junction of Donegall Street and Waring Street.

A Royal Avenue Northern Bank

B Four Corners

C Gordon Street in the Cathedral Quarter

D St Anne's Cathedral

Eastbank

Developments for the east bank of the River Lagan near the Odyssey Complex will include the rationalisation of the road system involving the removal of the current flyover. New apartment and office blocks are also planned for this site.

The Eastbank site, 2005

Custom House Square

The area in front of the historic Custom House has been refurbished by Laganside, creating an exciting outdoor venue for a range of events. The Square opened in April 2005.

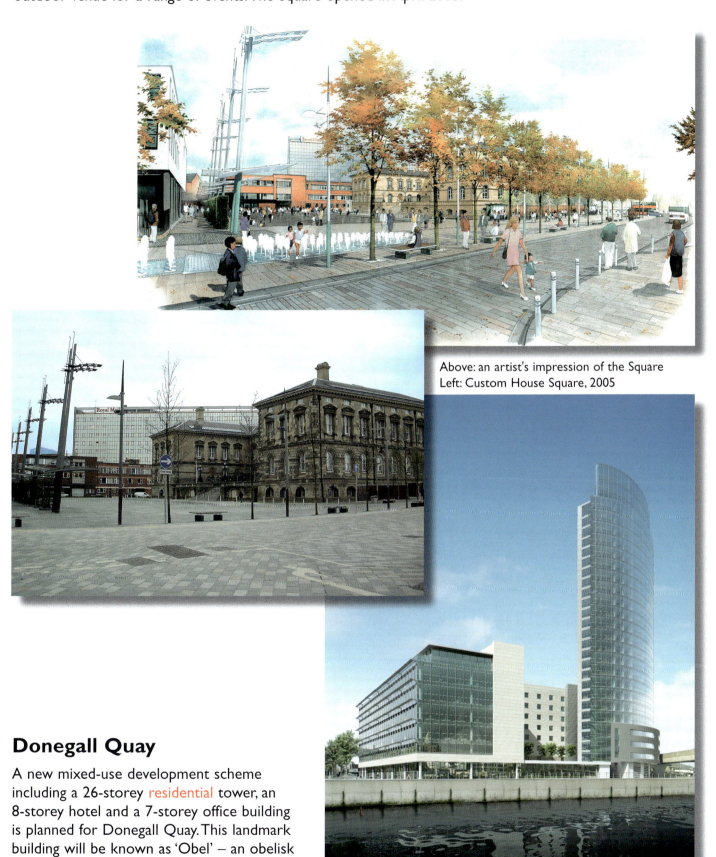

Above: an artist's impression of the Square
Left: Custom House Square, 2005

Donegall Quay

A new mixed-use development scheme including a 26-storey residential tower, an 8-storey hotel and a 7-storey office building is planned for Donegall Quay. This landmark building will be known as 'Obel' – an obelisk set in old Belfast.

A computer-generated image of what the 'Obel' will look like

Pathways

There are now 4.5 kilometres of pathways along the Lagan linking many of these sites.

Laganside estimates that over £800 million has been invested in the plan and that over 12 000 jobs have come into the area. Current office space exceeds 180 000 square metres and there are 700 housing units. We can also add the construction jobs created as the various schemes have been built, and we see that a lot of money has been put into the local economy in the last 16 years.

Walkway at Mays Meadow, 2001

Titanic Quarter

This is 75 hectares of brownfield land at Queen's Island formerly used for shipbuilding. It includes the slipway where the Titanic was launched in 1912 and the drawing offices where the ship was designed. It is prime development land fronting the River Lagan and is only 1.5 kilometres from the city centre.

The plans for the area include:
- Up to 3300 apartments and town houses
- 180 000 square metres of business/office space
- 130 000 square metres of light industry, showrooms and commercial development
- A Titanic Heritage Centre
- 2 hotels
- Leisure development – cafes, bars, restaurants, etc
- A cruise liner berth

The overall investment cost is in the region of £1 billion and it is hoped to provide around 20 000 new jobs in the area.

Sustainability

Governments and councils are coming to realise that we cannot go on using up the Earth's resources the way we are at present. We need to use resources on a more sustainable basis. Sustainability is one of the ways that planners will have to look at cities in the future. Cities will have to be planned so that we use less and recycle more of our waste. The pie charts (Resource L) show that Northern Ireland is lagging behind in the drive towards recycling waste from towns and cities.

Resource L ▶

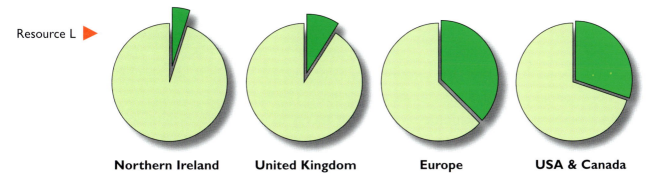

| Northern Ireland | United Kingdom | Europe | USA & Canada |

We need to recycle because we are producing more and more waste from homes, businesses and industries. Why is this? There are five reasons:

- There is an increasing population.
- Products are cheaper, so we buy more and replace more often.
- People have more money to spend.
- Products have more packaging.
- There are more convenience products.

The diagram on the right shows what the average domestic bin contains. ▶

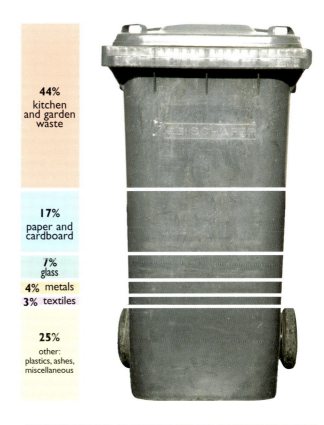

44% kitchen and garden waste

17% paper and cardboard

7% glass

4% metals

3% textiles

25% other: plastics, ashes, miscellaneous

In Northern Ireland we produce nearly 900 000 tonnes of waste every year. The bill for disposing of Belfast's waste is £8 million every year. Simply put, we are running out of landfill sites. Councils in Northern Ireland have been set targets to recycle more, and to send less waste to landfill sites (photograph A). The targets are as follows:

- Cut Biodegradable Municipal Waste (waste which can be composted, such as grass cuttings, potato peelings and dead flowers) sent to landfill sites by 25% in 2010
  50% by 2013
  65% by 2020
- By 2005 recover 25% of household waste
- By 2010 recover 40% of household waste

We will need to reduce what we use, reuse more, recycle more, recover more and dispose of less in landfills. There are a number of ideas that councils are considering.

A

1 We can recycle more of our waste in the council recycling depots such as the one run by Down District Council in Downpatrick.

| Bottle bank | Paper bank | Plastic bottles | Electrical goods | Biodegradable waste |

Bottle bank: one tonne of recycled glass saves one tonne of sand and limestone and cuts global warming.

Paper bank: one tonne of recycled paper saves cutting down 17 trees.

Plastic bottles: recycling one plastic bottle saves enough energy to light a bulb for 6 hours.

Electrical goods: each year we landfill 6 million items worth £50 million.

Biodegradable waste: this can be composted and sold to gardeners.

2 Some householders in the Down District Council area are provided with three separate bins for recycling some of their household waste at home (see photograph B).

3 We can bring in more kerbside recycling schemes where we separate the waste at home and put it into a separate box. These schemes take clean food cans, drinks cans, plastic bottles, newspapers, magazines, textiles, aluminium foil, glass bottles and jars, and thin cardboard. The box is collected weekly and the contents are hand sorted. Bryson House launched a trial scheme in 2001 and this has now expanded to 8 council areas covering 25% of the homes in Northern Ireland: – Belfast, Castlereagh, Banbridge, Armagh, Newtownabbey, Ballymena and Carrickfergus. As well as helping us to deal with increasing amounts of waste, recycling also:

- Saves raw materials
- Saves energy and fossil fuels
- Reduces greenhouse gases and helps to reduce global warming
- Provides up to 400 local jobs in recycling and recovery
- Reduces landfill, and means less landfill sites

Green transport

Transport will have to be planned so that we use less fossil fuels, make more use of public transport and put less emphasis on the motor car. Belfast, like most other MEDC urban areas, is very dependent on the car, but there are some green transport measures being introduced to encourage more people to leave their car at home.

Green transport measures like this will:

- Cut down on carbon emissions which are the main cause of greenhouse gases and global warming
- Help us to cut down on our use of expensive fossil fuels which have to be imported from overseas
- Lead to less pollution and a cleaner environment in our cities
- Help to ease traffic congestion in central Belfast
- Reduce the need for expensive road schemes to improve traffic flow

Bus lane on the Ormeau Road

Cycle route 93 at Fortwilliam

3.3 Measures to control traffic

The invention of the motor vehicle has been one of the major influences in the last hundred years. From the arrival of the first petrol-driven automobile in 1886 we reached a staggering 600 million vehicles in 2005. This rise has been greatest in MEDCs although many LEDC cities are also grinding to a halt as more and more vehicles pour onto the road. Resource M shows some of the increases associated with this problem.

Resource M ▼

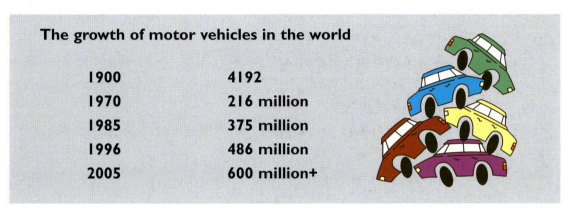

The growth of motor vehicles in the world

1900	4192
1970	216 million
1985	375 million
1996	486 million
2005	600 million+

Although we are going to concentrate on Paris, the problem is not unique to Paris. The following introduction could apply to any big city in Europe. Until the early years of the twentieth century changes were based round the needs of residents who were mainly pedestrians. Only the rich could afford to travel by carriage. Most goods were transported by horse and cart, canals or by rail. There was little or no forward planning and no overall authority coming up with plans for development. As the century wore on more and more people owned a car and soon the price fell until owning a car was within the reach of most people. As a result, in the late twentieth century it was realised in European cities that the uncontrolled growth of the motor vehicle industry could not continue, and they began to look at ways in which they could limit or control it. Unfortunately this proved easy to say, but hard to put into practice because people did not see why they should give up the cars they had worked so hard to get.

Too many vehicles in big cities lead to the following problems:
- Traffic jams, especially during the morning and evening rush hours
- Air pollution from exhaust fumes
- Loss of time and money as drivers sit in traffic jams going nowhere
- Increased costs to businesses and drivers
- Loss of trade and business as people avoid the affected area or move their businesses to quieter areas
- More road accidents – leading to more injuries, hold-ups and loss of money
- Increased pressure on emergency services
- Increased road rage and more accidents

There are a number of approaches to the problem which can be summed up as follows:

The traditional approach to the problem is to build your way out with more roads, extra lanes, flyovers, ring roads, urban motorways and other schemes designed to make life easier for the motorist. Some would argue that all this does is make things easier for a while so that more motorists come onto the roads and within three or four years the problem is as bad as ever.

A more radical approach is to make life more difficult for motorists and encourage them to leave their cars at home. This approach includes congestion charging, parking restrictions, increasing the price of petrol, traffic wardens, clearways, parking meters and limiting drivers to using their cars on certain days. This does not work either, as motorists will always find the extra money needed so that they have the luxury of driving their car when and where they want.

A third approach is to make public transport so attractive that people use it instead of using their cars. Measures include bus lanes; park and ride; metro lines; tramlines; integrating rail, metro and bus routes; and subsidised public transport.

In reality none of these approaches work in isolation and most cities use a mixture of all three.

Case study Paris

We will look at the problems in Paris in particular to see which of these approaches they use and how successful they have been.

Growth of Paris

Paris is the largest city in France and one of the largest in Europe. Even in 1851 it had over 3 million people and was the capital and centre of culture, politics, government and finance. It was also an important industrial centre. Greater Paris now has a population of over 11.1 million, of whom 2.1 million live inside the Boulevard Peripherique – the Inner Ring Road. The population density in this central area is over 13 000 per square kilometre.

Paris exerts a huge influence on France:

- This area generates 30% of France's GDP.
- There are over 5 million jobs in Paris.
- There are 1.6 million jobs in the centre of Paris, but 0.9 million of the workers live in the suburbs.
- Paris has 43 million square metres of office space.

The road network of France focuses on Paris like the spokes of a wheel. It is difficult to get from one part of France to another without going through Paris.

A defensive wall surrounded Paris. Inside the wall there was very little space and buildings were densely packed together. Many of the bigger roads in Paris met in huge open areas called 'Places'. Some of these had as many as 8 roads radiating out from them – the Arc de Triomphe area has 12! These were ideal for the nineteenth-century pedestrian as they gave excellent views of the fine buildings but they proved a problem for twentieth-century traffic. Try to imagine driving through Paris and meeting a roundabout with 12 roads! The first attempt to improve transport began when the first metro (underground railway) was opened in 1900. Metro lines only covered the city of Paris. They did not reach into the suburbs.

What has been done to try to solve the problem?

Apart from building the metro system very little was done. The population grew bigger and there was no regional, local or government planning until 1965. Meanwhile the number of cars increased forcing the authorities to spend huge amounts of money trying to solve the increasing traffic problems. This was because of the following facts:

- France builds 2 million cars every year.
- 70% of households in Paris own a car.
- The average speed of a car in Paris is 16 kilometres per hour.
- 53% of Parisians use a car daily.
- Only 35% use public transport.
- Cars are responsible for 75% of the city's pollution.
- 1.3 million vehicles circulate daily in Paris.
- Paris has 85% of France's traffic jams.
- 20 million tourists visit Paris every year.
- 56% of Parisians favour traffic limitation in the city centre.
- Paris has the highest rate of pollution of any European city.

Since then the following measures have been put into effect:

Metro

The French underground system, which was limited to the central area but has now been extended into the suburbs

- 14 lines, 9 of which extend into the suburbs
- 200+ kilometres of track
- 368 stations
- 1.2 billion passengers use it every year.
- Inside the Boulevard Peripherique you are no more than 600 metres from a station.

Réseau Express Régional (RER) lines

—— **A**
—— **B**
—— **C**
—— **D**
—— **E**

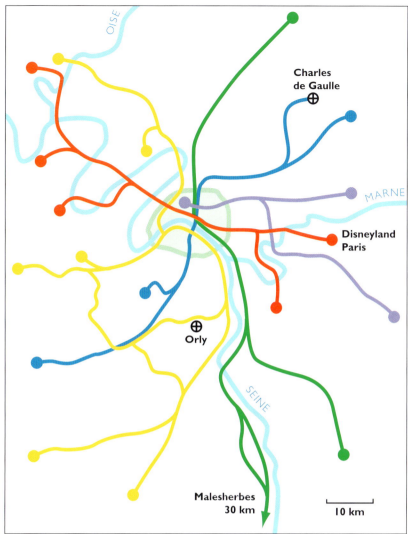

Charles de Gaulle

Disneyland Paris

Orly

Malesherbes
30 km

10 km

OISE

MARNE

SEINE

RER

This is a system of regional expressways built between 1960 and 1990. They go further out to the newer suburbs, to the two Paris airports and right through the centre of Paris.

- 5 lines
- An extra 102 kilometres of track
- 50 stations
- Over 300 million passengers per year

Tramways

Fully automated and linking up the suburbs to each other.
- 2 lines
- 20 kilometres of track
- 33 stations
- 35 000 passengers per day

Bus routes

- 7500 buses
- 1100 routes
- 70 strategic routes using newer faster 'Mobilien – Bus Network Modernisation Programme' buses, with a 45% increase in passengers
- Waiting time under 10 minutes
- Bendy buses on main routes
- Bus lanes which are kerbed off so that car drivers cannot use them
- Over 1 billion passengers per year

Ticketing

- Annual, monthly and weekly passes with up to 50% discounts
- Integrated ticketing system – tickets can be used on buses, trams, RER and metro
- 3-day and 5-day tickets for tourists

Boulevard Peripherique

An inner ring road of motorway standard
- 35 kilometres in length
- 34 intersections
- 2 million cars using it every day

========= **All underground**
(to be completed in 2007)

BP **Boulevard Peripherique**

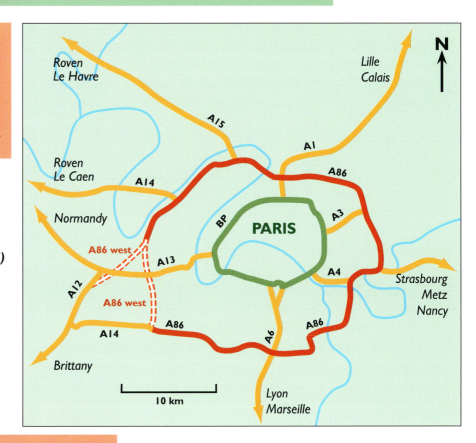

A86 motorway

An outer ring motorway designed to take through traffic round Paris and not into the centre
- 80 kilometres
- Over 40 intersections
- Links all the main motorways coming into Paris

Other methods

The mayor of Paris stated in 2001 that he would "fight with all the means at [his] disposal, against the harmful, ever-increasing and unacceptable hegemony of the motor car." Since then he has tried the following ideas:

- Reduced some main roads from 3 lanes to 2 and put in bus and cycle lanes
- Turned 2 kilometres of the Pompidou Expressway into a beach for a month in summer. This runs along the side of the River Seine and gives Parisians a chance to relax, sunbathe and party on a beach in the middle of Paris, hence its name – 'Paris Plage'. See photographs C, D and E.
- Removed all free parking spaces (see photograph B)
- 'Greened' areas close to the centre by banning cars, blocking off streets and cutting speed limits to 30 kilometres per hour (20 miles per hour)
- Put in 197 kilometres of cycle tracks with plans for another 300 kilometres by 2010
- Increased the price of diesel
- Brought in overall speed restrictions in the heat wave summer of 2003 to reduce ozone levels
- Introduced car free days when all roads into Paris were blocked

- Introduced 'Axes Rouge' – key roads into and through Paris where any stopping or parking is forbidden. These rules are strictly enforced and cars are towed away. See photograph A.

© François Nonnenmacher, Paris

The future

In recent years there have been proposals to further improve the public transport network as follows:
• Another 60 kilometres of tramlines which will form a ring round Paris – 'The Rocade Grand Tram' (€0.39 billion)
• 4 more metro extensions into the suburbs (€0.62 billion)
• 8 new multi modal exchanges where passengers can switch easily from one form of transport to another, eg tram to bus or bus to metro (€0.19 billion)
• Creation of more suburban railways linking the main suburbs with each other (€0.88 billion)

How successful has Paris been in solving its traffic problems?

Despite having the best public transport system in Europe, and spending billions of francs and euros the French love affair with the car continues:

- From 1991 to 1997 the number of car trips in the Paris region increased from 14 million to over 17 million.
- The number of trips by public transport stayed at 6.6 million.
- Over 70% of all journeys in Paris still involve the use of a car.

The problem is summed up as follows:

Sacre bleu, mon ami! If more people switched to public transport then there would be less traffic on the roads and my journey to work in my car would be a lot easier!

There is no city with a population of over 0.5 million that has cut congestion just by improving public transport.

Like every other city in Europe it is doubtful if the government has the will to tackle the problem properly. Any government that proposes laws to limit the car will be voted out at the next election.

Questions

1 Study the table which shows statistics for three settlements in County Londonderry, and answer the questions below. The number of marks for each question is given. Questions with one mark have a one word answer. In questions with two or three marks you would be expected to write two or three lines.

Settlement	Eglinton	Dungiven	Ballykelly
Population (2001 census)	3150	2988	1827
Primary schools	2	3	2
Post primary schools	0	2	0
Low order shops & services	16	33	16
High order shops & services	6	30	7
Churches	2	3	3
Banks	1 cashpoint	2	1 cashpoint

Eglinton

Dungiven

Ballykelly

(a) Which settlement has the largest population? (1)

(b) How many schools are there in Eglinton? (1)

(c) What is the total number of shops and services in Ballykelly? (2)

(d) State and explain one reason why Dungiven has two post primary schools. (3)

(e) "Larger settlements have more services than smaller settlements." Using evidence from the table, state whether you agree or disagree with this statement and give a reason for your answer. (2)

2 Study Resource N which shows a kerbside recycling box in the Willowfield district of Belfast. Answer the following questions.

Resource N ▶

(a) Why is this called a kerbside recycling scheme? (2)

(b) Give two reasons why schemes like these have been introduced into Northern Ireland. (4)

(c) Study the following list and underline items which would be suitable for collecting in a kerbside recycling box.

newspapers	clean food tins	food waste	aluminium drink cans
magazines	grass cuttings	cardboard	hot ashes

(5)

3 Study Resource O, which shows an aerial photograph of Belfast Harbour. The area of Titanic Quarter is outlined in red. Answer the questions which follow.

(a) Match up the following features with the correct letter from the photograph.

River Lagan   ...

Odyssey   ...

Abercorn Basin   ...

Harland & Wolff cranes   ...

Waterfront Hall   ...

Bridge   ...

Area of housing   ...

Park   ...   (8)

(b) The area marked X on the photograph is a brownfield site. What is a brownfield site?   (2)

(c) There are plans to develop light industry on this site. State and explain two reasons why this would be a suitable site for industry.   (6)

(d) The area marked Y is the Eastbank site which is to be developed by Laganside. There are plans to build houses and apartments on this site. State and explain two reasons why this would be a suitable site for housing.   (6)

(e) Name one group who might oppose the development of housing on the site.   (2)

(f) State and explain one reason why they might oppose the development of housing.   (3)

(g) Look at the bridge marked Z. Read the following statements about this bridge and say whether they are true or false.

This is the lowest bridging point on the River Lagan.

The bridge is upstream of the Eastbank site.

This is the highest point of navigation on the River Lagan.   (3)

Resource O

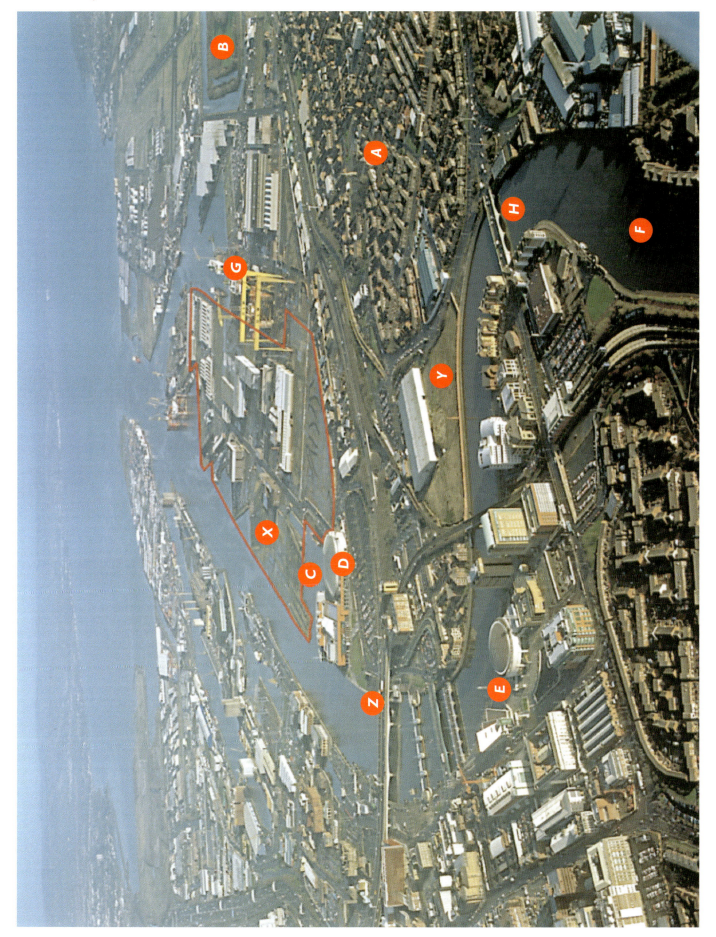

Fieldwork

There is a requirement for candidates to submit one item of coursework. This should be an enquiry investigation relevant to their course of study which is supported by fieldwork. Some schools give pupils a range of fieldwork and allow them to choose their own topic, while others decide on a topic which will be attempted by a group of pupils who collect and pool their information. There are a number of ideas which can be used and developed by teachers and pupils. These are briefly summarised as follows:

- **Theme A** gives pupils the opportunity to measure elements of weather over a period of time, eg maximum–minimum temperature, precipitation, wind speed and direction, cloud cover, cloud type and pressure. Results can be compared with local or national forecasts to determine their accuracy, or they can be obtained from different parts of the school environment to study the micro-climate effect. A more difficult proposition is to collate the data from a particular farm and try to see how the weather affects the farming activities.

- **Theme B** gives opportunities for pupils to look at river processes (see photograph A). Measurements can be taken for width, depth, speed, discharge, gradient, slope of banks, size of load at various points and shape of load (angular, sub angular or rounded). The study can be done from source to mouth on one river, two rivers can be compared, or one river could be studied at different seasons.

- **Theme C** could be tied in to Theme B by studying pollution in rivers. Pupils could investigate levels of lead, phosphates, nitrates, pH levels, dissolved oxygen, biological survey or temperature. This type of investigation might suit a pupil with a scientific background. A further idea for investigation is a quadrat survey of a particular ecosystem such as farmland or blanket bog at various heights (see photograph B).

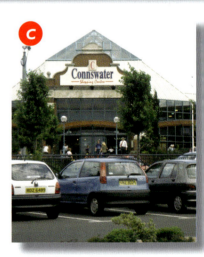

- **Theme D** could look at migration in an area of a town or a small settlement. A questionnaire might help pupils to find out the percentage of residents who were born there, and where the migrants came from and why. This would tie in to push–pull factors. A more difficult study would be to work out population pyramids for a number of small areas and to compare them!

- **Theme E** might lend itself to a study in an urban area which looked at changes in land use, by comparing old maps with the current situation on the ground. Pupils could also attempt to compare an area or a settlement in terms of economic activity (primary, secondary, tertiary).

- **Theme F** gives pupils a chance to attempt a number of investigations, such as looking at the urban field of a settlement, shopping centre or even an individual shop (see photograph C). Questionnaires can be used to see how far shoppers will come, how they travel, how often they visit, and what they buy. It is also possible to delineate a CBD by measuring the pedestrian flow, looking at rateable values, or looking at the number of storeys in buildings. A more difficult study would ask pupils to survey a number of settlements in an area, and to attempt to put them in a hierarchy by population and/or services.

Glossary and Index

Soil	A mixture of weathered rock, humus and minerals, which forms the outer layer of the Earth's crust. *21, 56, 70–72, 78, 83, 89, 92, 95–97, 110, 114, 138*
Sustainable	Development which does not exploit resources more rapidly than the renewal of those resources. *70, 87, 100–101, 106, 113–114, 119, 141*

GLOSSARY – Theme D

Birth rate	The number of babies born per thousand people per year. *89, 98–99, 105, 123*
Death rate	The number of people dying per thousand people per year. *89, 98, 123*
Migration	Movement of people from one area/country to another. *89, 95, 97–99, 123, 158*
Non-renewable	Resources which cannot be replaced once they run out, such as coal or oil. *100*
Population distribution	The way in which the population is spread out over an area. *88–91, 94–95*
Population density	A measure of population in people per square kilometre. *88, 91, 93, 127, 146*
Population pyramid	A diagram which shows the breakdown of the population by age and sex. Also called an age–sex pyramid. *98–99, 105, 158*
Population structure	The way in which a population is made up. *98*
Renewable	Resources which can be used over and over again such as wood or fish. *100–101, 103–104, 116*
Resource	Something dug, quarried or taken from the Earth or sea, which can be used by man. *88, 97, 100, 104, 106, 143*

GLOSSARY – Theme E

Appropriate technology	Technology which is given to an LEDC which is appropriate to their level of development. *113–114, 116*
Brownfield site	An area for building which has been built on before but is now derelict. *109, 134, 142, 156*
Footloose	An industry which has no particular requirements for location. *112*
Greenfield site	An area for building which has never been built on before. *109, 134*
Hi-tech industry	Industries which have grown up in the late twentieth century based on high technology and computers. *112*
Industrial location	The reasons why an industry locates in a particular place. *108, 112*
Primary activity	Jobs which obtain the raw materials or resources which we need. *60, 108, 110, 119, 158*
Secondary activity	Jobs which make the raw material into something useful that we need. *60, 97, 108–109, 119, 158*
Tertiary activity	Jobs which provide a service for other industries. *108–110, 119, 158*
Traditional industry	Industries which grew up and located in a country in the late nineteenth and early twentieth centuries such as steel, shipbuilding and linen. *112*

GLOSSARY – Theme F

CBD	Central Business District – the area at the centre of a city, a zone of business, commerce and entertainment. *69, 125, 129, 131–132, 137, 139, 158*
Commuter settlement	Settlements containing a large number of commuters – people who live some distance from their employment and have to travel to and from work every day. *126*
Counterurbanisation	The movement of people from a large urban area back to the countryside. *89, 120, 124, 126*
Functional zones	The zones in a city which are divided up according to their function or use, eg housing, recreation, industry or commerce. *129*
Green belt	The area around a settlement where new building is subject to strict planning controls. *124, 129, 131, 134–135*
Hierarchy	An arrangement which puts settlements in order according to their size. *127–128, 158*
Location	The place where a settlement grew up in relation to the surrounding countryside/area. *120, 122, 129*
Planning	The process by which government attempts to control what happens in a particular area, zone or city. *62, 107, 120, 134–135, 145, 147*
Residential	Land used mainly for housing. *129, 141*
Rural	To do with the countryside. *27, 45, 123*
Settlement	A place where people live. *22, 45, 91, 120–123, 126–131, 134–135, 155, 158*
Site	The actual place where a settlement grew up. *62, 76, 101, 107, 109–110, 112, 120, 122, 134, 138–139, 140, 142, 156*
Sphere of influence	The area round a settlement from which people will travel to that settlement for goods and services. *128*
Urban	To do with villages, towns or cities. *27, 89, 97, 112, 120, 122–123, 125, 127–128, 135, 144, 146, 158*
Urbanisation	The movement of people from outlying rural areas into large cities or urban areas. *97, 120, 122–124*